MW01048891

Emily Dickinson

Emily Dickinson

SINGULAR POET

Carol Dommermuth-Costa

Lerner Publications Company • Minneapolis

To my mother, Yolanda,
my late father, Peter,
and to my stepfather, Joe Reynolds,
with gratitude for their love and support

Library binding by Lerner Publications Company
A division of Lerner Publishing Group
241 First Avenue North
Minneapolis, MN 55401 U.S.A.

website address: www.lernerbooks.com

Library of Congress Cataloging-in-Publication Data

Dommermuth-Costa, Carol.
    Emily Dickinson : singular poet / by Carol Dommermuth-Costa.
        p. cm.
    Includes bibliographical references (p.) and index.
    Summary: Examines the life, work, and significance of the
visionary poet from Amherst, Massachusetts.
    ISBN 0-8225-4958-1 (alk. paper)
    1. Dickinson, Emily, 1830–1886—Biography—Juvenile
literature. 2. Women poets, American—19th century—Biography
—Juvenile literature. [1. Dickinson, Emily, 1830–1886. 2. Women poets,
American. 3. Poets, American. 4. Women—Biography.] I. Title.
PS1541.Z5D59 1998
811'.4—dc21
    [B]   97–40081

Manufactured in the United States of America
2 3 4 5 6 7 – JR – 05 04 03 02 01 00

Contents

1   *I'm Nobody! Who Are You?*   7

2   *I Am Growing Handsome Very Fast Indeed*   17

3   *I Cared Less for Religion Than Ever*   29

4   *My Life Was Made a Victim*   41

5   *I'll Tell You What I See Today*   55

6   *The Mind Is So Near Itself*   65

7   *I Find Ecstasy in Living*   75

8   *I Confess that I Love Him*   85

9   *Blow Has Followed Blow*   97

Sources 106

Bibliography 107

Index 110

Amherst College, right, *set the small town of Amherst,* seen beyond, *apart from other small towns in New England.*

 ONE

I'm Nobody! Who Are You?

1830–1839

Amherst, Massachusetts, in the mid-1800s was a tidy little town surrounded by patches of farmland. The bookstore carried several newspapers and only those books considered by the community to be good, wholesome reading. There were a few general stores and a Congregational Church, and most of Amherst's citizens built their homes on one of two streets: Main Street or North Pleasant Avenue.

There were no railroads in Amherst. People went from place to place by horse and buggy or in horse-drawn cabriolets, fancy carriages. They used candles and gas lamps to light their homes and streets. The townspeople needed little from the outside world. Many families grew their own vegetables and fruit. Some even raised chickens and cows, which provided them with eggs, cheese, and milk. Most kitchens had a pump for water, but the bathrooms were outside.

Amherst was like other small towns on the East Coast, with two exceptions: it had a college and it had a mystery. The college was aptly called Amherst College. The mystery was in the form of a woman named Emily Dickinson.

Many stories had grown up around Amherst's mysterious woman. Some said that she wrote beautiful poems about nature and feelings and she didn't share them with anyone but her sister. Others said that Miss Dickinson hadn't been out of her house for fifteen years, except for one night when she crept outside to take a quick glimpse of the church in the moonlight. They said she stayed in seclusion because she was nursing a broken heart from a love that was lost. Newcomers to the town said that Miss Dickinson didn't really exist. They said she was a myth the townspeople had created in order to make their own town seem extraordinary.

But the children of the town knew that if they went to play near the Dickinson house, they would soon see a basket of sweets being lowered from one of the upstairs windows. And if they looked very carefully, they could just make out a figure in white behind the curtain. One time, they found a scrap of paper lying among the sweets. It was a poem that read

> I'm Nobody! Who are you?
> Are you—Nobody—Too?
> Then there's a pair of us!
> Don't tell! they'd advertise us—you know!
>
> How dreary—to be—Somebody!
> How public—like a Frog—
> To tell one's name—the livelong June—
> To an admiring Bog!

Emily Dickinson was indeed a real person. She was a woman with a soft, gentle voice. She was a writer and a poet, and she was very shy. Emily was happiest spending her life in her house and the surrounding gardens. Because of her solitary life, she found time to connect with her feelings and write poetry that people would read and love for years to come.

The Dickinson family had lived in Amherst for four generations. Emily's grandfather, Samuel Fowler Dickinson, had helped found Amherst College in 1821. The college consisted of two buildings with dormitories where students from out of town could live while completing their course of study.

Amherst College was originally established to prepare men for the ministry. By the time Emily's father, Edward, attended the college, however, its program included other areas of study.

It was not an easy task to keep a college financially sound, and Samuel Fowler Dickinson struggled for years to keep Amherst College open. By 1830 he was on the verge of bankruptcy. Amherst College almost closed that year.

In order to conserve money, the Dickinson family all moved in together. They lived in a large red brick house on Main Street called the Homestead. Samuel Fowler Dickinson, his wife Lucretia, and their younger children lived in one half of the house. Edward, his wife Emily Norcross Dickinson, and their son Austin lived in the other half, which was separated by a common hallway and stairs leading to the second floor. Emily Elizabeth Dickinson was born in the Homestead on December 10, 1830.

A comfortable white porch, supported by four huge columns, ran along the front of the Homestead. A barn sat on the property, as well as a shed for the family carriage and a huge woodpile to fuel the stove and fireplace. On the side of

The Homestead, where Emily was born, was shared by Emily's parents and grandparents.

the house there were apple, pear, cherry, and peach trees, a vegetable garden, and another beautiful garden that displayed flowers of infinite variety. A conservatory, or greenhouse, separate from the house allowed the family to enjoy fresh flowers all year long.

Unfortunately, in the midst of all the beauty at the Homestead, a great deal of turmoil existed when Emily was a baby. Her grandfather, tired of the financial strain it took to keep Amherst College open, decided to give up the fight. In 1833, when Emily was two years old, Samuel Fowler Dickinson took his wife and their youngest child, Elisabeth, and moved to Ohio.

Edward Dickinson was just starting his practice as a lawyer. He barely made enough money to support a large house and a family. He was also burdened with the financial responsibility of supporting his brother Frederick along with Frederick's wife and two children. This financial pressure filled the whole household with anxiety.

Then Emily's mother, Emily Norcross Dickinson, found that she was expecting a third child. She was very sick and couldn't care for both three-year-old Austin and two-year-old Emily. Mrs. Dickinson asked her sister Lavinia if Emily could live with her for a while. So Emily was sent away to stay with her aunt, who lived about thirty miles from Amherst.

Aunt Lavinia wrote to Mr. Dickinson about her young niece:

> Emily is perfectly well and contented—She is a very good child & but little trouble—She has learned to play on the piano—she calls it the moosic. She does not talk much about home—sometimes speaks of little Austin but does not moan for any of you—She has a fine appetite & sleeps well & I take satisfaction in taking care of her. . . .
>
> I took her to meeting yesterday morning—She behaved very well—Once in a while she would speak loud but not to disturb any one—she sit between Pa and me—he would slap her a little occasionally when she was doing wrong—not to hurt her or make her cry—

After a year with her aunt, Emily was returned to her home. Her younger sister, Lavinia, had been born, and her mother had recovered enough to care for all three children.

In 1835, when Emily was four years old, she started school in a two-story whitewashed brick building on Pleasant Street. The students all used the same textbook, the *New England Primer,* which taught them not only to read and write but to live a good life so they would go to heaven when they died. Emily learned to read from this book, which was filled with prayers and religious rhymes. She had to memorize the prayers and say them regularly. One of the bedtime prayers taught Emily that there was a connection between sleeping and death:

> I in the burying place may see
> Graves shorter there than I:
> From death's arrest no age is free—
> Young children too may die.
>   My God, may such an awful sight
> Awakening be to me!
> O! that by early grace I might
> For death prepared to be!

One of the rhymes that Emily memorized on how to live a good life read

> I must obey my Lord's commands
> Do something with my little hands . . .
> Young Samuel that little child,
> He served the Lord, liv'd undefil'd . . .
> While Eli's wicked children dy'd . . .
> These good examples were for me;
> Like these good children I must be.

It was unusual, in 1835, for a girl of Emily's age to attend school. But it was Mr. Dickinson's wish that she do so. Emily's father once wrote a series of articles for the Amherst newspaper outlining the proper roles that women and men should have in society. He believed that girls should be educated as well as boys, if they chose. Although women spent their lives raising a family and taking care of a household, he saw an educated woman as an asset to her husband. He also believed that a woman had no place in business or politics but could best fulfill her role in life by having children and taking care of the home.

Emily's mother seemed to fit Mr. Dickinson's idea of the perfect woman. She was well educated, yet she put most of her energy into keeping an efficient home and being a hospitable hostess to her husband's clients and guests.

Edward Dickinson and Emily Norcross Dickinson, as they looked when Emily was a child

Emily never thought of her mother as a woman of education. She saw her as a quiet, frail woman who seemed to have little time or desire for intellectual pursuits. Mrs. Dickinson often suffered from ill health, usually brought about by her husband's long absences from home. Mr. Dickinson had to travel to Washington a great deal, and when he was away for more than a week, Emily's mother became very depressed and took to her bed.

The lack of attention and affection was very difficult for Emily. It was different from the lavish affection that had been showered on her as a toddler by her Aunt Lavinia. This lack of attention was probably what prompted Emily to say years later: "I never had a mother. I suppose a mother is one to whom you hurry when you are troubled."

Even though Mr. Dickinson showed little affection toward his children, Emily adored her father. He read the Bible to Austin, Emily, and Vinnie every morning and led them in their prayers every night. He was very strict and set in his ways. Emily rarely saw him smile, and his tone of voice could be gruff and impatient. When he was displeased with something Emily said or did, he would show his displeasure with stony silence. Even so, Emily missed him when he was away. In letters to Mr. Dickinson, Emily's mother expressed how much Emily and Austin missed their father:

> January 7, 1838 . . . The children are well . . . They are very desirous I should say to their father they have been good children. Emily sais she wishes I would write to you that she should be glad to see you but she hopes it is all for the best that you are away.

> January 21, 1838 . . . The children are well except Emily she had not been as well as usual, for a week I think however she is much better now. I have not let

her go to school more than two or three days since you left. She speaks of her Father with much affection. She sais she is tired of living without a father.

March 20, 1838 . . . The children send much love and wish very much for their dear Father's return.

Emily was an outgoing child, and she had many friends. One of her favorite playmates was Helen Fiske. Helen, Emily, and Vinnie loved to hunt for berries and chestnuts. The girls spent a lot of time outdoors, and Emily developed a love and appreciation of nature. She spoke to the robins in the morning and to the orioles nesting in the cherry trees. Each spring, Emily watched patiently for the daffodils to come up under the apple trees. She developed a special sense of the beauty of nature and of the relationship between nature and humans. Unlike children who found their joy in worldly things, Emily discovered her joy in the beauty and harmony of the natural world.

This portrait of Emily, Austin, and Vinnie was painted in 1840.

TWO

I Am Growing Handsome Very Fast Indeed

1840–1846

In 1840, when Emily was nine years old, Mr. Dickinson decided to move his family to a larger house in Amherst. His law practice was doing well, and he felt that his family would benefit from living in a larger space. He bought a house on Pleasant Street, across from Emily's school.

Emily was old enough to attend Amherst Academy, a school for girls. The course of study at the academy was intense, and it challenged Emily's mind. She studied arithmetic, grammar, composition, ancient history, chemistry, astronomy, anatomy, logic, and Greek. Amherst Academy was religiously oriented, so all the subjects were taught from a religious perspective. Students at the academy were encouraged to attend lectures at Amherst College as a way of enriching their course of study.

Emily enjoyed studying at the academy, and she made friends easily. Her friendships with four other girls was what made school the most fun. Abiah Root, Abby Wood, Harriet

Emily made many friends while she was a student at Amherst Academy.

Dickinson, Sarah Tracy, and Emily made up a club called the Unseen Trap, which met in a forest grove near the academy. There they wrote letters to each other, made up funny stories and jokes about some of the teachers in school, and shared confidences. They also went to parties together and wrote entertaining verses on St. Valentine's Day.

Emily made other friends, including Mattie and Sue Gilbert, Jane Humphrey, and Emily Fowler. Emily Fowler was the granddaughter of Noah Webster, the originator of the first dictionary.

Emily was taught that letter writing was considered a practice of self-improvement, a way of perfecting grammar, spelling, and written expression. Emily took letter writing seriously—writing drafts of her letters and then revising and polishing them before sending them off. She sometimes included poems in her letters, and she wrote to her friends as often as possible. Her brother, Austin, became Emily's first correspondent.

Both Emily and Vinnie adored their older brother. Emily was especially troubled when he left Amherst in the spring of 1842 to attend Williston Seminary, a boarding school in East-hampton. Emily found that writing to Austin shortened the distance between them.

> 18 April 1842
>
> My dear brother
>
> As Father was going to Northampton and thought of coming over to see you I thought I would improve the opportunity and write you a few lines— We miss you very much indeed you cannot think how odd it seems without you there was always such a Hurrah wherever you was. . . . we received your letter Friday morning and very glad we were to get it you must write oftener to us the temperance dinner went off very well the other day all the Folks Except Lavinia and I there were over a Hundred there the students thought the dinner too cheap the tickets were a half a dollar a piece and so they are going to have a supper tomorrow Evening which I suppose will be very genteel. . . . Charles Richardson has got back and is in Mr Pitkins store Sabra is not running after him at all she had not seen him when I last saw her which was Saturday I suppose she would send her *respects to you* if *she knew I was going to write* to you—I *must now close*—all send a great deal of love to you and hope you are getting along well and—Enjoy your self—
>
> Your affectionate Sister Emily—

Jane Humphrey graduated from Amherst Academy a year before Emily. After Jane had left Amherst, Emily began corresponding with her friend. The girls shared their concerns about school, teachers, friends, and their looks.

12 May 1842

My dear Jane

I have been looking for a letter from you this long time but not receiving any I plucked up all the remaining courage that I had left and determined to make one more effort to write to you a few lines—I want to see you very much for I have got a great deal to tell you about school matters—and besides you are one of my dear friends. Sabra has had a beautiful ring given to her by Charles you know who as well as I do—the Examination at Easthampton is today—and Austin is coming home tonight. Father is sick with the Rheumatism and can not go but Mother has gone with somebody else—it is very unpleasant today—it showers most all the time. . . . I miss you more and more every day, in my study in play at home indeed every where I miss my beloved Jane—I wish you would write to me—I should think more of it than of a mine of gold—when you write me I wish you would write me a great long letter and tell me all the news that you know of—all your friends send a great deal of love to you. . . . what good times we used to have jumping into bed when you slept with me. I do wish you would come to Amherst and make me a great long visit—how do you get along in Latin. . . . I can think of nothing more to say now yours affectionately

Emily

Abiah Root only attended Amherst Academy for nine months, but she and Emily formed a fast friendship. The two girls continued to correspond. Emily wrote:

23 February 1845

Dear Abiah,

—After receiving the smitings of conscience for a long time, I have at length succeeded in stifling the voice of that faithful monitor by a promise of a long letter to you; so leave everything and sit down prepared for a long siege in the shape of a bundle of nonsense from friend E.

. . . I keep your lock of hair as precious as gold and a great deal more so. I often look at it when I go to my little lot of treasures, and wish the owner of that glossy lock were here. Old Time wags on pretty much as usual at Amherst, and I know of nothing that has occurred to break the silence; however, the reduction of the postage has excited my risibles somewhat. Only think! We can send a letter before long for five little coppers only, filled with the thoughts and advice of dear friends. But I will not get into a philosophizing strain just yet. There is time enough for that upon another page of this mammoth sheet. . . . Your *beau ideal* D. I have not seen lately. I presume he was changed into a star some night while gazing at them, and placed in the constellation Orion between Bellatrix and Betelgeux. I doubt not if he was here he would wish to be kindly remembered to you. . . .

I do wish you would come, 'Biah, and make me a long visit. If you will, I will entertain you to the best of my abilities, which you know are neither few nor small. Why can't you persuade your father and mother to let you come here to school next term, and keep me company, as I am going? Miss—, I presume you can guess who I mean, is going to finish her education next summer. The finishing stroke is to be put on at [Norton]. She will then have learned all that we poor foot-travellers are toiling up the hill of knowledge to acquire. Wonderful thought! Her horse has carried her along so swiftly that she has nearly gained the summit, and we are plodding along on foot after her. Well said and sufficient this. We'll finish an education sometime, won't we? You may then be Plato, and I will be Socrates, provided you won't be wiser than I am. . . . All the girls send much love to you. And please accept a large share for yourself.

From your beloved
Emily E. Dickinson.

[P. S.] Please send me a copy of that Romance you was writing at Amherst. I am in a fever to read it. I expect it will be against my Whig feelings.

7 May 1845

Dear Abiah,

It seems almost an age since I have seen you, and it is indeed an age for friends to be separated. I was delighted to receive a paper from you, and I also was much pleased with the news it contained, especially that you are taking lessons on the "piny," as you always call it. But remember not to get on ahead of me. Father intends to have a piano very soon. How happy I shall be when I have one of my own! . . . Viny [Vinnie] went to Boston this morning with father, to be gone a fortnight, and I am left alone in all my glory. I suppose she has got there before this time, and is probably staring with mouth and eyes wide open at the wonders of the city. I have been to walk to-night, and got some very choice wild flowers. I wish you had some of them. . . . My plants look finely now. I am going to send you a little geranium leaf in this letter, which you must press for me. Have you made you an herbarium yet? I hope you will if you have not, it would be such a treasure to you; 'most all the girls are making one. If you do, perhaps I can make some additions to it from flowers growing around here. How do you enjoy your school this term? Are the teachers as pleasant as our old school-teachers? I expect you have a great many prim, starched up young ladies there, who, I doubt not, are perfect models of propriety and good behavior. If they are, don't let your free spirit be chained by them. I don't know as there [are] any in school of this stamp. But there 'most always are a few, whom teachers look up to and regard as their satellites. . . .

I had so many things to do for Viny, as she was going away, that very much against my wishes I deferred writing you until now, but forgive and forget, dear A., and I will promise to do better in future. Do write me soon, and let it be a long, long letter; and when you can't get time to write, send a paper, so as to let me know you think of me still, though we are separated by hill and stream. All the girls send much love to you. Don't forget to let me receive a letter from you soon. I can say no more now as my paper is all filled up.

Your affectionate friend,
Emily E. Dickinson

When Emily was alone, one of her favorite pastimes was reading, even though most of her reading had to be done privately when she was at home. Mr. Dickinson did not approve of reading, except books of a religious nature. He believed that "reading joggled the Mind." The Congregational Church, which played a large role in Amherst, also taught that reading was a bad influence on the minds of young people.

Austin and Emily shared books with each other, and Austin was one of Emily's ongoing correspondents.

But both Emily and Austin loved to read, and they often sneaked books into their rooms for what they called "reading feasts." Emily also encouraged her friends to read. In time, the girls formed the Shakespeare Club. Each month they would decide on a book to read, and then they would get together to talk about the book. They discussed how much they liked the book, what the characters were like, and if they agreed with the way the author depicted the characters and resolved the story.

Emily, Austin, and their friends also traded books. Friends would drop books off at the Dickinson house by way of the bushes along the porch.

Emily was a sociable teenager. She loved parties and meeting new people. And she was becoming aware of the fact that young men found her attractive. In a letter written to Abiah in 1845, Emily shared a certain pride in her looks with her friend.

> I am growing handsome very fast indeed! I expect I shall be the belle of Amherst when I reach my 17th year. I don't doubt that I shall have perfect crowds of admirers at that age. Then how I shall delight to make them await my bidding, and with what delight shall I witness their suspense while I make my final decision.

Emily didn't limit her friendships to school friends, however. She enjoyed spending time with the young men who worked at her father's office and with Austin's friends. Her mind was always open and inquiring, and she enjoyed discussing politics, business, and literature.

Although her studies at the academy kept her very busy, Emily still had time for weekly piano and singing lessons. She became quite proficient at playing several tunes, such as "The

Grave of Bonaparte" and "Maiden, Weep No More," which were popular at the time.

In April 1845, when Emily was fourteen years old, her school friend Sophia Holland died. Sophia's death made a lasting impression on Emily, and it took years for her to come to terms with it. It wasn't until a year later that she could write to Abiah about Sophia's death:

> My friend was Sophia Holland. She was too lovely for earth & she was transplanted from earth to heaven. I visited her often in sickness & watched over her bed. But at length Reason fled and the physician forbid any but the nurse to go into her room. Then it seemed to me I should die too if I could not be permitted to watch over her or even to look at her face. At length the doctor said she must die & allowed me to look at her a moment through the open door. I took off my shoes and stole softly to the sick room.
>
> There she lay mild & beautiful as in health & her pale features lit up with an unearthly—smile. I looked as long as friends would permit & when they told me I must look no longer I let them lead me away. I shed no tear, for my heart was too full to weep, but after she was laid in her coffin & I felt I could not call her back again, I gave way to a fixed melancholy.

Emily's sadness was so deep that her mother suggested she leave Amherst for awhile. Emily decided to visit her Aunt Lavinia, who had moved to Boston.

In September 1846, Emily boarded the train for Boston. What excitement she felt! It was the first time she had ever traveled alone. Her aunt and two cousins, aware of Emily's grief over Sophia's death, attempted to lift her out of her melancholy. They felt that the best way to do this was to keep Emily busy, and Boston was the place to do this.

The sights were almost endless: Bunker Hill, museums,

concerts, and botanical gardens, which were a special pleasure to Emily. By the end of the month, Emily had somewhat recovered her old gaiety, although she still missed Sophia deeply.

When Emily returned home from Boston, she decided to undertake a new project—a botanical book. Botany, the study of plants and flowers, was a subject that Emily had studied at the academy. She had also been newly encouraged by the botanical exhibitions and lectures she had attended in Boston. Emily spent the next few weeks exploring the woods near her home.

Primroses and heliotrope, jasmine and gillyflowers, mignonette and sweet alyssum—they were all gathered into Emily's apron and brought home. She spent hours drying the flowers and mounting them into a bound book. Emily carefully wrote the name of each flower, first in Latin and then in

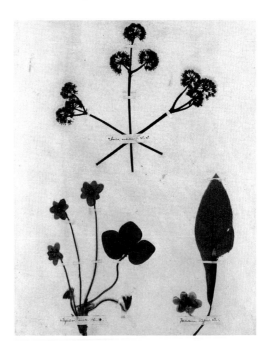

When Emily was fifteen, she made an herbarium, a book filled with dried flowers.

English. By the time she had completed her project, over four hundred different varieties of flowers were exhibited in her book, her herbarium.

Emily continued to write. Some of her poems wove together her love of nature and her deepest feelings.

> "Nature" is what we see—
> The Hill—the Afternoon—
> Squirrel—Eclipse—the Bumble bee—
> Nay—Nature is Heaven—
> Nature is what we hear—
> The Bobolink—the Sea—
> Thunder—the Cricket—
> Nay—Nature is Harmony—
> Nature is what we know—
> Yet have no art to say—
> So impotent Our Wisdom is
> To her Simplicity.

Emily tried to understand nature by using her favorite things to describe it. She was a bit frustrated with trying to define just what goes into making up nature, yet she found that it was profound in its simplicity. This deep respect for and appreciation of the beauty and variety of Mother Nature continued to influence her writing.

In the late 1800s, revival meetings were held all over New England.

 THREE

I Cared Less for Religion Than Ever

1847–1849

One day, sixteen-year-old Emily wrote to her friend Abiah about revival meetings that had taken place in Amherst a few days before:

> The meetings were thronged with people old and young.... It was really wonderful to see how near heaven came to sinful mortals. Many who felt there was nothing in religion determined to go once & see if there was anything in it, and they were melted at once.... I attended none of the meetings last winter.... I felt that I was so easily excited that I might again be deceived and I dared not trust myself.

Revival meetings blew like tornadoes across every small town in New England at that time. They were held every few years for the express purpose of reviving people's religious fervor. During these meetings, preachers graphically depicted the horrors of hell and the bliss of heaven. Everyone was a sinner, the preachers loudly proclaimed, and unless

29

people confessed their sins and took refuge in God, they would suffer the fires of damnation.

The threat of eternal damnation was not taken lightly by God-fearing people. Death at a young age was a frequent occurrence in the 1800s. Diseases such as pneumonia, tuberculosis, and smallpox were common. Drinking water was often contaminated, and death from cholera and typhoid was not unusual. The complications from a simple cold could result in death. For those who survived their youth, the average adult life span was still only fifty-five. The reminder of death was all around, and everyone wanted to be assured that their life after death would be better than their life on earth.

Life in Amherst in the 1800s centered around religion. Mrs. Dickinson and many others like her believed in a judgmental God who meted out punishment if people didn't do things to make him happy. She believed that if misfortune befell herself or her family, it was because God was showing his displeasure. Mr. Dickinson was also a devout member of the church. He read the Bible each night to his family, and he wanted to be thought of as a God-fearing man in his community.

By the time Emily was sixteen years old, she had begun to discard the religion of her community and parents. She stopped attending church services and revival meetings, because she believed in a benevolent God. Emily saw the presence of the Creator in everything, especially in nature.

The Murmur of a Bee
A Witchcraft—yieldeth me—
If any ask me why—
'Twere easier to die—
Than tell—

The Red upon the Hill
Taketh away my will—
If anybody sneer—
Take care—for God is here—
That's all.

The Breaking of the Day
Addeth to my Degree—
If any ask me how—
Artist—who drew me so—
Must Tell!

One by one, Emily's friends were converted, but she resisted. She wrote to Abiah: "I soon forgot my morning prayer or else it was irksome to me. One by one my old habits returned and I cared less for religion than ever."

Emily took a firm stand with her family. She patiently listened to the Bible readings and attended an occasional church service with her parents. But she refused to get involved in the religious activities of the community.

In 1847, Emily enrolled in the Mount Holyoke Female Seminary in South Hadley, Massachusetts, along with about three hundred other young women. There were three levels —junior, middle, and senior. Sixteen-year-old Emily entered as a junior.

Emily was homesick. She missed her family and friends, but she also missed the intellectual atmosphere of her home and family. She was used to a life in which she was treated as an intellectual equal by those years older than herself. Reading the newspapers had been her way of keeping up with the local and national news, and she could hold her own in any

Students stroll on the grounds in front of Mount Holyoke Female Seminary.

discussion, especially a political discussion, with Austin's friends. In fact, most of her intellectual contacts had been with boys and men.

At Mount Holyoke, she felt the loss of male companionship. She felt at times as though she was being intellectually stifled by the religious and feminine atmosphere of the school. She wrote to Austin with humor and sarcasm about her frustrations—especially feeling separate from life outside of Mount Holyoke.

> South Hadley, 21 October 1847
> My dear Brother. Austin.
> . . . Won't you please to tell me . . . who the candidate for President is? I have been trying to find out ever

since I came here & have not yet succeeded. I dont
know anything more about affairs in the world, than
if I was in a trance, & you must imagine with all your
"Sophomoric discernment," that it is but little & very
faint. Has the Mexican war terminated yet & how?
Are we beat? Do you know of any nation about to be-
siege South Hadley? If so, do inform me of it, for I
would be glad of a chance to escape, if we are to be
stormed. I suppose Miss Lyon. would furnish us all
with daggers & order us to fight for our lives, in case
such perils should befall us. . . .

Your aff. Emily

By early November, Emily had adjusted to Mount
Holyoke. She had a busy schedule, which ensured that she
wouldn't have too much idle time on her hands in which to be
homesick. She wrote to her friend Abiah, giving her a picture
of the Mount Holyoke school year and schedule:

South Hadley, 6 November 1847

My dear Abiah.

I am really at Mt Holyoke Seminary & this is to
be my home for a long year. Your affectionate letter
was joyfully received & I wish that this might make
you as happy as your's did me. It has been nearly six
weeks since I left home & that is a longer time, than
I was ever away from home before now. I was very
homesick for a few days & it seemed to me I could not
live here. But I am now contented & quite happy, if I
can be happy when absent from my dear home &
friends. You may laugh at the idea, that I cannot be
happy when away from home, but you must remember that I have a very dear home & that this is my first
trial in the way of absence for any length of time in my
life. . . .

The school is very large & though quite a number have left, on account of finding the examinations
more difficult than they anticipated, yet there are

nearly 300 now. Perhaps you know that Miss. Lyon is raising her standard of scholarship a good deal, on account of the number of applicants this year & on account of that she makes the examinations more severe than usual. . . .

I room with my Cousin Emily, who is a Senior. She is an excellent room-mate & does all in her power to make me happy. You can imagine how pleasant a good room-mate is, for you have been away to school so much. Everything is pleasant & happy here & I think I could be no happier at any other school away from home. Things seem much more like home than I anticipated & the teachers are all very kind & affectionate to us. They call on us frequently & urge us to return their calls & when we do, we always receive a cordial welcome from them.

I will tell you my order of time for the day, as you were so kind as to give me your's. At 6. oclock, we all rise. We breakfast at 7. Our study hours begin at 8. At 9. we all meet in Seminary Hall, for devotions. At 10¼. I recite a review of Ancient History, in connection with which we read Goldsmith & Grimshaw [authors of History texts]. At .11. I recite a lesson in "Pope's Essay on Man" which is merely transposition. At .12. I practice Calisthenics & at 12¼ read until dinner, which is at 12½ & after dinner, from 1½ until 2 I sing in Seminary Hall. From 2¾ until 3¾. I practise upon the Piano. At 3¾ I go to Sections, where we give in all our accounts for the day, including, Absence—Tardiness —Communications—Breaking Silent Study hours— Receiving Company in our rooms & ten thousand other things, which I will not take time or place to mention. At 4½. we go into Seminary Hall, & receive advice from Miss. Lyon in the form of a lecture. We have Supper at 6. & silent-study hours from then until the retiring bell, which rings at 8¾, but the tardy bell does not ring until 9¾, so that we dont often obey the first warning to retire.

Unless we have a good & reasonable excuse for failure upon any of the items, that I mentioned above, they are recorded & a *black mark* stands against our names. . . . My domestic work is not difficult & consists in carrying the Knives from the 1st tier of tables at morning & noon & at night washing & wiping the same quantity of Knives. I am quite well & hope to be able to spend the year here, free from sickness . . . .

Abiah, you must write me often & I shall write you as often as I have time. But you know I have many letters to write now I am away from home. Cousin Emily says "Give my love to Abiah."

From your aff
Emily E. D—

In addition to the academic schedule, two thirty-minute periods were allotted each day for meditation and prayer, which suited Emily quite well. She enjoyed her quiet times alone where she could think and meditate on life and its connections to the Creator.

Mount Holyoke Seminary was run by a young scholar and devout Christian, Mary Lyon. Miss Lyon took it upon herself to save the souls of the young students that passed through the halls of her school. She had founded the seminary to lead the students to a faith in Christ and to enlist their help in saving a lost world.

Miss Lyon constantly reinforced these beliefs both by her teachings and her kindnesses to all of her students. She made sure that the other teachers did likewise. Emily once commented on this in a letter to Abiah: "One thing is certain & that is, that Miss. Lyon & all the teachers, seem to consult our comfort & happiness in everything they do & you know that is pleasant."

Miss Lyon was well liked by the students of Mount Holyoke. She instilled in her young women sound virtues of discipline, honesty, and a strong self-will, in addition to solid Christian beliefs. She was dedicated to giving her students the best education she could. Her favorite expression was: "We may become almost what we will"—if one had the will to accomplish something, anything was possible.

The students at Mount Holyoke were permitted to go home for Thanksgiving. Emily's brother and father drove to pick her up from school, and she noted the tears in her mother's eyes as she came in the door. She had a great time while she was at home for the holiday, and she missed the warmth and coziness of her home more than ever when she returned to school. After seeing friends and family at Thanksgiving, she didn't want to leave home ever again.

Emily returned to her arduous schedule, however, and continued to excel in her studies. But by the time Christmas came, she was once again terribly homesick. And Christmas not being a family holiday as much as a religious observance, the students were not permitted to go home.

On Christmas Eve, Miss Lyon announced that Christmas Day would be celebrated with fasting and prayer. That meant that the girls were not allowed out of their rooms for the day. They were to go without meals, and they were to spend the time praying.

After making her pronouncement to the assembly of young women, Miss Lyon asked all to stand as an acknowledgment of their commitment to the spiritual agenda that she had just mapped out for them. Every student in the school stood up—except Emily and her cousin. Then Miss Lyon said that any student who did not agree with the program of the day and wished to spend the day otherwise should stand up. As the students looked around, Emily was the only one to be seen, defiantly standing among her seated classmates.

Fearing a reprimand from Miss Lyon and homesick for family life, Emily decided to board a stagecoach home to

Amherst. Her family was shocked and appalled at her behavior, but Emily wouldn't admit to doing anything wrong. She had just stood up, quite literally, for what she believed in.

Mr. Dickinson wrote a hasty letter to Miss Lyon, apologizing in Emily's behalf and asking for Miss Lyon's understanding. Miss Lyon agreed to take Emily back, apparently seeing her as the ultimate challenge in her religious crusade to save young women's souls.

In February 1849, Miss Lyon lectured the girls on the foolishness of valentine cards. She told them that sending valentines was expressly forbidden and anyone caught doing so would be severely reprimanded.

Again, Emily decided that Miss Lyon was not going to dictate to her. She enlisted the aid of the postmaster at South Hadley. More than 150 valentine cards went out from Mount Holyoke, all of them sent by Emily.

In March 1849, Emily developed a hacking cough. Because a severe cough could turn into pneumonia and death, Mr. Dickinson decided that Emily would heal faster at home under her mother's care. A month later, when Emily was on the road to recovery, she was allowed to continue her studies at home.

Her convalescence was a great opportunity for her to read books and poems other than those required by the school. Austin gave his sister a copy of Henry Wadsworth Longfellow's popular romantic novel *Kavanagh*. He became one of Emily's favorite poets, as did Elizabeth Barrett Browning. Emily also read the novels of Charlotte and Emily Brontë.

As Emily's health improved, she spent time with her friends going for long walks in the woods. They were always amazed at her familiarity with the wild plants that grew there. After returning to school, Emily wrote to Abiah of the two great pleasures she had experienced while at home in Amherst:

>   South Hadley, 16 May 1848
> My dear Abiah,
> . . . The older I grow, the more do I love spring and spring flowers. Is it so with you? While at home there were several pleasure parties of which I was a member, and in our rambles we found many and beautiful children of spring, which I will mention and see if you have found them, —the trailing arbutus, adder's tongue, yellow violets, liver-leaf, blood-root, and many other smaller flowers.
>   What are you reading now? I have little time to read when I am here, but while at home I had a feast in the reading line, I can assure you. Two or three of them I will mention: *Evangeline* [a poem by Henry Wadsworth Longfellow], *The Princess* [by Alfred, Lord Tennyson], *The Maiden Aunt* [by Marcella Bute Smedley], *The Epicurean* [by Thomas Moore], and *The Twins and Heart* by Tupper, complete the list. Am I not a pedant for telling you what I have been reading? . . .
>   Ever your own affectionate
>   Emilie E. Dickinson.

Mr. Dickinson decided Emily would not continue her schooling after the spring term was over. Emily had mixed feelings after hearing that this would be her final semester at Mount Holyoke. On the one hand, she was happy to be going home. There was a part of her, however, that regretted that she had not succumbed to becoming a formal Christian, as most of her friends had. She wrote to Abiah:

> Father has decided not to send me to Holyoke another year, so this is my *last term*. . . . It startles me when I really think of the advantages I have had, and I fear I have not improved them as I ought. . . . I regret

that last term, when that golden opportunity was mine, that I did not give up and become a Christian. It is not now too late, so my friends tell me, so my offended conscience whispers, but it is hard for me to give up the world.

In August 1849, Emily left Mount Holyoke for good. Seven months later, in March 1850, Mary Lyon died. Emily read the obituary notice in the newspapers and looked back with fondness on a woman who had taught her so much about herself. Many years later, Emily would write the following poem. Perhaps she was thinking of Mary Lyon when she wrote it.

> I went to thank Her—
> But She Slept—
> Her Bed—a funneled Stone—
> With Nosegays at the Head and Foot—
> That Travellers—had thrown—
>
> Who went to thank Her—
> But She Slept—
> 'Twas Short—to cross the Sea—
> To look upon Her like—alive—
> But turning back—'twas slow—

When Emily was in her late teens, a silhouette was made of her.

FOUR

My Life Was Made a Victim

1850–1854

The year 1850 was witness to the election of Millard Fillmore, the thirteenth president of the United States; the famous Compromise of 1850 between proslavery and antislavery factions in the country; and the introduction of hoop skirts for women and bowler hats for men. While all these things were making news, Emily was reading about them in the newspapers.

No less than fifteen different publications were delivered monthly to the Honorable Edward Dickinson, Box 207, Amherst—the formal address of Emily's home. Publications such as the *Observer, New England Farmer,* and the *Boston Courier* were read by all members of Emily's family. With four newspapers, three religious magazines, three literary magazines, and two publications dealing with law and politics, the Dickinson household was kept well informed about the important developments of their day.

Emily also had an excellent collection of books in her home. Mr. Dickinson's library was filled with books of poetry and classics carefully selected to reflect only those that he considered fit reading for people both young and old. Emily chose to read the novels of Charles Dickens, the poems of Alfred, Lord Tennyson and Henry Wadsworth Longfellow, and the essays of philosopher and writer Ralph Waldo Emerson.

Charlotte Brontë was Emily's favorite author. Brontë's novel *Jane Eyre,* published a few years earlier in 1847, was becoming popular. It was not the type of book that Mr. Dickinson would have had in his library. He would have felt that the free and independent lifestyle lived by the heroine would only serve to give Emily "ideas." But a young clerk in her father's law office had read the book and told Emily about it. She asked to borrow it and probably read it without her father's knowledge. She kept the book for three months, and read it several times. She loaned it to her friend Sue Gilbert, and they spent hours discussing the book.

Emily felt a special bond with the heroine of the book, Jane Eyre. She felt that, in some ways, she and Jane were similar. Emily was close to Jane in age—Jane was eighteen and Emily nineteen. Emily also shared some of Jane's physical characteristics—she had a small build and an interesting but plain face. In the book, Jane expressed a wish to look different than she did, to be prettier, taller—qualities Emily herself wished for. And Jane Eyre was high-spirited and adventurous—qualities used to describe Emily.

Emily differed from Jane, however, in the way she lived her life. While Jane lived a life consistent with an adventurous nature, Emily lived quietly in Amherst, rarely venturing forth from the little town. Reading about Jane Eyre may have made Emily long for a more independent lifestyle, one in which she was free to come and go as she pleased.

At nineteen, Emily was old enough to be married and have children, yet she was still being treated as a child by her family, especially by her father. Her brother moved to Boston, but whenever Emily tried to become more independent, she was reprimanded for it.

In May 1850, Emily wrote to Abiah, confiding her frustration. When she desperately wanted to go riding with a friend, she felt she couldn't leave her mother and her duties.

> 7 and 17 May 1850
>
> Dear Remembered.
> ... When I am not at work in the kitchen, I sit by the side of mother, provide for her little wants—and try to cheer, and encourage her. I ought to be glad, and grateful that I *can* do anything now, but I do feel so very lonely, and so anxious to have her cured. I hav'nt repined but *once,* and you shall know all the why. While I washed the dishes at noon in that little "sink-room" of our's, I heard a well-known rap, and a friend I love *so* dearly came and asked me to ride in the woods, the sweet-still woods, and I wanted to exceedingly—I told him I could not go, and he said he was disappointed—he wanted me very much—then the tears came into my eyes, tho' I tried to choke them back, and he said I *could,* and *should* go, and it seemed to me unjust. Oh I struggled with great temptation and it cost me much of denial, but I think in the end I conquered. ...
>
> I went cheerfully round my work, humming a little air till mother had gone to sleep, then cried with all my might, seemed to think I was much abused, that this wicked world was unworthy such devoted and terrible sufferings, and came to my various senses in great dudgeon at life, and time, and love for affliction, and anguish. ...
>
> Your aff friend,
> Emily.

Emily had a curfew, and her father was adamant that she maintain it. One night when she was out visiting with friends,

Emily arrived home at nine o'clock to find her father furious with her. She was so upset that she decided to leave home, but she changed her mind. That evening, she wrote to Austin:

> Father [was] in great agitation at my protracted stay —and mother and Vinnie in tears, for fear that he would kill me. . . . I put on my bonnet tonight, opened the gate very desperately, and for a little while the suspense was terrible—I think I was held in check by some invisible agent, for I returned to the house without having done any harm!

When Mr. Dickinson was at home, he demanded that all the letters that Emily received and sent be read to the family. This lack of privacy bothered Emily. She wrote to Austin:

> I received what you wrote, at about 2½ oclock yesterday. Father brought home the same, and waited himself in order to have me read it—I reviewed the contents hastily—striking out all suspicious places, and then very *artlessly* and unconsciously began. My heart went "pit a pat" till I got safely by a remark concerning Martha, and my stout heart was *not* till the manuscript was over. The allusion to Dick Cowles' grapes, followed by a sarcasm on Mr Adams' tomatoes, amused father highly.

In 1850, George Gould, editor of the Amherst College newspaper, *The Indicator,* published one of Emily's valentines in the February issue. The valentine combined both prose and poetry, and it was unusually long for a valentine verse. It began:

> Magnum bonum, "harum scarum," zounds et zounds, et war alarum, man reformam, life perfectum, mundum changum, all things flarum?

Sir, I desire an interview; meet me at sunrise, or sunset, or the new moon—the place is immaterial. In gold, or in purple, or sackcloth—I look not upon the *raiment* [clothing]. With sword, or with pen, or with plough—the weapons are less than the *wielder* [the one who carries them]. . . . With soul, or spirit, or body, they are all alike to me. With host or alone, in sunshine or storm, in heaven or earth, *some* how or *no* how—I propose, sir, to see you. . . .

The Indicator listed the author of the poem as "anonymous." But a comment accompanied the poem: "I wish I knew who the author is. I think she must have some spell, by which she quickens the imagination, and causes the high blood 'run frolic through the veins.'"

Emily loved to try her hand at writing valentines. It was common for young women of Amherst to use valentine writing as a way to show off their knowledge of literature. In 1852, one of Emily's whimsical valentine poems was published in the *Springfield Daily Republican,* a western Massachusetts newspaper read by people across the country.

"*Sic transit gloria mundi,*"
  "*How doth the busy bee,*"
"*Dum vivimus vivamus,*"
  I stay mine enemy!

Oh, "*veni, vidi, vici!*"
  Oh caput, cap-a-pie!
And oh "*memento mori*"
  When I am far from thee!

Hurrah for Peter Parley!
 Hurrah for Daniel Boone!
Three cheers, sir, for the gentleman
 Who first observed the moon!

Peter, put up the sunshine;
 Patti, arrange the stars;
Tell Luna *tea* is waiting,
 And call your brother Mars!

Put down the apple, Adam,
 And come away with me,
So shalt thou have a *pippin*
 From off my father's tree! . . .

Good bye, Sir, I am going;
 My country calleth me;
Allow me, Sir, at parting,
 To wipe my weeping e'e.

In token of our friendship
 Accept this "Bonnie Doon,"
And when the hand that plucked it
 Hath passed beyond the moon,

The memory of my ashes
 Will consolation be;
Then, farewell, Tuscarora,
 And farewell, Sir, to thee!

As talented as Emily was at writing light, sentimental, or silly valentine poems, she was also skilled at writing serious poetry. She wrote the following poem in 1853:

> On this wondrous sea
> Sailing silently,
> Ho! Pilot, ho!
> Knowest thou the shore
> Where no breakers roar—
> Where the storm is o'er?
>
> In the peaceful west
> Many the sails at rest—
> The anchors fast—
> Thither I pilot thee—
> Land Ho! Eternity!
> Ashore at last!

Emily often shared her poems with people whom she knew would support her, such as Benjamin Newton, a friend and an apprentice in her father's law office. Emily also exchanged poems with Henry Vaughan Emmons, a student at Amherst College, and Joseph Lyman, a friend of both Emily and Austin. Emily's friend Sue Gilbert was also a great support. Like Emily, Sue was well educated and intelligent, and the two women were close friends. At Emily's request, Sue often critiqued Emily's poems.

In September 1852, Sue accepted a teaching job in Baltimore, Maryland. Emily was devastated at losing the constant company of her friend.

In her letters to Sue, Emily expressed the intense depths of feeling for Sue. Emily almost seemed to have been in love with Sue, and although Sue felt a deep affection for Emily, it seemed as though the intensity was one-sided.

> Will you let me come dear Susie—looking just as I do, my dress soiled and worn, and my grand old apron, and my hair—Oh Susie, time would fail me to enumerate my appearance, yet I love you just as dearly as if I was e'er so fine, so you wont care, will you? I am so glad dear Susie—that our hearts are always clean, and always neat and lovely, so not to be ashamed. I have been hard at work this morning, and I ought to be working now—but I cannot deny myself the luxury of a minute or two with you.
>
> The dishes may wait dear Susie—and the uncleared table stand, *them* I have always with me, but you, I have "not always"—*why* Susie, Christ hath saints *manie*—and I have *few,* but thee—the angels shant have Susie—no—no no! . . . Oh my darling one, how long you wander from me, how weary I grow of waiting and looking, and calling for you; sometimes I shut my eyes, and shut my heart towards you, and try hard to forget you because you grieve me so, but you'll never go away, Oh you never will—say, Susie, promise me again, and I will smile faintly—and take up my little cross again of sad—*sad* separation. How vain it seems to *write,* when one knows how to feel— how much more near and dear to sit beside you, talk with you, hear the tones of your voice. . . . Only *want* to write me, only sometimes sigh that you are far from me, and that will do, Susie. . . . Love always, and ever, and true!
>
> Emily—

In another letter to Sue Gilbert, Emily poured out more of her heart. In the first sentence of the letter, she quoted from Longfellow's poem "The Rainy Day."

Emily cared passionately for Sue Gilbert.

It's a sorrowful morning Susie—the wind blows and it rains; "into each life some rain must fall," and I hardly know which falls fastest, the rain without, or within—Oh Susie, I would nestle close to your warm heart, and never hear the wind blow, or the storm beat, again. Is there any room there for me, or shall I wander away all homeless and alone? Thank you for loving me, darling, and *will* you "love me more if ever you come home"?—It is enough, dear Susie, I know I shall be satisfied. But what can I do towards you?— *dearer* you *cannot* be, for I love you so already, that it almost breaks my heart—perhaps I can love you *anew,* every day of my life, every morning and evening—Oh if you will let me, how happy I shall be!

The precious billet [letter], Susie, I am wearing the paper out, reading it over and o'er, but the dear *thoughts* cant wear out if they try, Thanks to Our Father, Susie. Vinnie and I talked of you all last evening long, and went to sleep mourning for you, and pretty soon I waked up saying "Precious treasure, thou art

mine," and there you were all right, my Susie, and I
hardly dared to sleep lest some one steal you away.
Never mind the letter, Susie; you have so much to do;
just write me every week *one line,* and let it be,
"Emily, I love you," and I will be satisfied!

Your own Emily

In the spring of 1853, Emily was suffering pangs of loneliness. Sue was still in Baltimore, Austin was in Boston, and
many of her childhood friends were no longer part of her life.
Jane Humphrey had become a teacher and lived outside
Amherst. Emily Fowler, Abiah Root, and Abby Wood had become engaged and married. Other friends, such as Jennie
Grout and Martha Kingman, had fallen ill and died. Emily's
social circle was becoming smaller and smaller with each
passing year.

One day in January 1854, Emily was on her way to church
when suddenly and without warning a feeling of terror came
over her. She couldn't find any reason for the fear, but it was
something that made her run for her life. In a letter to Sue,
Emily described the event:

I'm just from meeting, Susie, and as I sorely
feared, my "life" was made a "victim." I walked—I
ran—I turned precarious corners—One moment I
was not—then soared aloft like Phoenix, soon as
the foe was by—and then anticipating an enemy
again. . . . I reached the steps, dear Susie. . . . How
big and broad the aisle seemed, full huge enough
before, as I quaked slowly up—and reached my
usual seat! . . . and there I sat, and sighed, and
wondered I was scared so, for surely in the whole
world was nothing I need to fear—Yet there the
Phantom was.

Emily felt a sense of mortal danger. But she didn't know
what the danger was from, since she realized that "in the

whole world was nothing I need to fear." The "Phantom" was what caused her fear, but she could not identify what it was.

Emily went on to tell Sue that she became calmer by the end of the church service, and she was content to walk home with her sister, Vinnie. Even then, she was a bit anxious:

> Until our gate was reached, and I needn't tell you Susie, just how I clutched the latch, and whirled the merry key, and fairly danced for joy, to find myself at *home!*

Emily experienced a fear that was more terrifying than anything she had ever known. But she recognized that there was nothing around her that should cause her to experience this terror. She felt as though she had gone out of her body or ceased to exist—for "one moment I was not." Because of her fear, she felt as if she were totally alone in the world.

Emily suffered from an emotional disorder called anxiety or panic disorder. Many people, especially women, became victims of this disorder. At the time, doctors had little knowledge of this problem, and they simply termed it "female nerves."

When someone has a panic attack in a certain place, they are frightened that if they return to that place, they will have the same terrifying experience. So Emily decided not to attend church anymore. She was afraid of repeating the terror she experienced on her way to church that day in January.

A few months later, some of Emily's loneliness was lifted when Sue Gilbert returned to Amherst. Sue and Emily tried to renew the intimate friendship that they had before Sue had left. But something was different.

Emily was hurt that her friend hadn't written quite as often as she would have liked. Sue, on the other hand, felt that Emily was too possessive with their friendship. Also, Sue was a devout churchgoer, and Emily no longer went to church. These differences led to a huge argument between the two friends. Finally, Emily wrote her friend a letter in which she expressed her feelings about the future of their relationship:

> Sue—you can go or stay—There is but one alternative—We differ often lately, and this must be the last.
>
> You need not fear to leave me lest I should be alone, for I often part with things I fancy I have loved, —sometimes to the grave, and sometimes to an oblivion rather bitterer than death—thus my heart bleeds so frequently that I shant mind the hemorrhage, and I only add an agony to several previous ones. . . .
>
> Few have been given me, and if I love them so, that for *idolatry,* they are removed from me—I simply murmur *gone,* and the billow dies away into the boundless blue, and no one knows but me, that one went down today. We have walked very pleasantly— Perhaps this is the point at which our paths diverge —then pass on singing Sue, and up the distant hill I journey on.

> I have a Bird in spring
> Which for myself doth sing—
> The spring decoys.
> And as the summer nears—
> And as the Rose appears,
> Robin is gone.
>
> Yet do I not repine
> Knowing that Bird of mine
> Though flown—
> Learneth beyond the sea
> Melody new for me
> And will return.

Fast in a safer hand
Held in a truer Land
Are mine—
And though they now depart,
Tell I my doubting heart
They're thine.

In a serener Bright,
In a more golden light
I see
Each little doubt and fear,
Each little discord here
Removed.

Then will I not repine,
Knowing that Bird of mine
Though flown
Shall in a distant tree
Bright melody for me
Return.

The rift between the friends did not last long. In following letters, Emily continued to express her longing to be with Sue. At the time, Sue was being courted by Austin. By the end of 1954, Sue and Austin had begun to speak of marriage, with the idea of getting married in the autumn of 1855. Although some of the intimacy was lost in Emily and Sue's relationship, Emily was happy to have Sue as a future sister-in-law.

Vinnie, above, *and Emily had a marvelous time in Washington, D.C. Over the years, Vinnie became Emily's support and comforter, more of an older sister than younger.*

FIVE

I'll Tell You What I See Today

1855–1859

In early February 1855, Emily and Vinnie left on a trip to Washington, D.C. This was the longest distance Emily had ever traveled from home. She and Vinnie were to spend three weeks in the nation's capital visiting their father. Since Mr. Dickinson's election to Congress in 1852, he had spent a great deal of time traveling back and forth between Amherst and Washington.

Mr. Dickinson was too busy with his congressional duties to take his daughters around the city, so Emily and Vinnie took themselves to see the sights. The two sisters also stopped off in Philadelphia on their return trip home. Emily wrote to Elizabeth Holland, a woman she had met a few years earlier and with whom she had formed a close friendship. Emily told about her visit to the nation's capital:

> Philadelphia, 18 March 1855
> Dear Mrs. Holland and Minnie, and Dr. Holland too . . .

I am not at home—I have been away just five weeks today, and shall not go quite yet back to Massachusetts. Vinnie is with me here, and we have wandered together into many new ways.

We were three weeks in Washington, while father was there, and have been two in Philadelphia. We have had many pleasant times, and seen much that is fair, and heard much that is wonderful—many sweet ladies and noble gentlemen have taken us by the hand and smiled upon us pleasantly—and the sun shines brighter for our way thus far.

I will not tell you what I saw—the elegance, the grandeur; you will not care to know the value of the diamonds my Lord and Lady wore, but if you haven't been to the sweet Mount Vernon, then I *will* tell you how on one soft spring day we glided down the Potomac in a painted boat, and jumped upon the shore —how hand in hand we stole along up a tangled pathway till we reached the tomb of General George Washington, how we paused beside it, and no one spoke a word, then hand in hand, walked on again, not less wise or sad for that marble story. . . .

Now, my precious friends, if you won't forget me until I get home, and become more sensible, I will write again, and more properly. Why didn't I ask before, if you were well and happy?

Forgetful
Emilie.

Emily and Vinnie enjoyed their trip, although Emily had refused to go at first. She was always uncomfortable about leaving her home—almost as if something terrible would happen.

In April 1855, Mr. Dickinson bought the Homestead, the house in which Emily had been born. Carpenters and painters worked for several months readying the house for the Dickinson family, and in November, they moved in. The Homestead provided all the solitude Emily could wish for in which to write her poems.

It was a difficult move, however, as Emily indicated in one of her letters soon after the family was settled in their new home. But Emily displayed humor in the face of a tough situation.

> Your voice is sweet, dear Mrs. Holland—I wish I heard it oftener. . . .
>
> I cannot tell you how we moved. I had rather not remember. I believe my "effects" were brought in a bandbox, and the "deathless me," on foot, not many moments after. I took at the time a memorandum of my several senses, and also of my hat and coat, and my best shoes—but it was lost in the melee, and I am out with lanterns, looking for myself . . . .
>
> From your mad
Emilie

Emily's life in her new home didn't change much after the move. Chores were an important part of every household, and the Dickinson home was no exception. Emily's chores included everything from baking bread daily to sweeping the kitchen, making the beds, and washing the floors on her hands and knees.

The kitchen was one of Emily's favorite rooms in the house. It was a cheerful room with pale green walls interrupted by yellow window casements. The many windows allowed the sunlight to shine into the room on bright, pleasant days.

Cooking and baking bread were some of Emily's favorite chores. A friend once commented that: "She makes all the bread, for her father only likes hers." Emily's rye-and-indian bread was so delicious that it took second prize at the 1856 Amherst Agricultural Fair. Emily's gingerbread was also a favorite in the Dickinson household.

Part of Emily's day was spent in the conservatory that lay next to the main house. There she nurtured herbs, wildflowers, and other delicate varieties of flowers. She also spent at least one hour each day of the summer tending the lush vegetable garden on the side of the house.

Emily loved being outside. She would sit amidst the flowers and grasses, deeply experiencing the richness of each season as it came and went. In April 1856, Emily wrote about her delight in the outdoor world to her cousin John Graves:

> It is Sunday—now—John—and all have gone to church—the wagons have done passing, and I have come out in the new grass to listen to the anthems.
>
> Three or four Hens have followed me, and we sit side by side—and while they crow and whisper, I'll tell you what I see today, and what I would that you saw—
>
> . . . the crumbling elms and evergreens—and *other* crumbling things—that spring, and fade, and cast their bloom within a simple twelvemonth— well—*they* are *here,* and skies on me fairer far than Italy. . . . And here are Robins—just got home—and giddy Crows—and Jays. . . . here's a *bumblebee*—not such as *summer* brings—John—ernest, manly bees, but a kind of a Cockney, dressed in jaunty clothes. . . . then there are *sadder* features—here and there, *wings* half gone to dust, that fluttered so, last year—a mouldering plume, an empty house, in which a bird resided. Where last year's flies, their errand ran, and last year's *crickets* fell!

Emily spent a good deal of time working on her poetry. She used any scrap of paper that was lying around to jot down the ideas that would enter her head at any given moment of the day. She wrote on the back of recipes and wrapping paper and in the margins of old newspapers. Finally Emily began to collect her poems into little booklets. She painstakingly folded and sewed together pieces of paper to form a book. Then she would write one poem on each page.

In 1856, Austin married Sue Gilbert. In order to keep the family close by, Mr. Dickinson built a house next door to the Homestead. He called it the Evergreens because it was surrounded by immensely tall, ancient evergreen trees. Austin and Sue moved in soon after their wedding.

It was wonderful for Emily to have both her brother and her dear friend living next door. The Evergreens also became a social center where Austin and Sue hosted parties. It was there that Emily made the acquaintance of Ralph Waldo Emerson, an essayist and philosopher and the founder of the Transcendentalist Movement. Harriet Beecher Stowe, the author of *Uncle Tom's Cabin,* also visited the Evergreens from time to time, as did Frederick Law Olmstead, the landscape architect who designed Central Park in New York City and Amherst's town square.

It was at one of these events at her brother's house that Emily met Samuel Bowles, the editor and sole writer of the *Springfield Daily Republican.* Sam Bowles often visited not only Austin's home but Emily's as well.

Sam was a handsome, charming man who was known for his appreciation of creative, intelligent women. He found both characteristics in Emily. He and Emily began to write letters to each other. She also sent him many of her poems. Even though he had published one of her valentines several years earlier, Sam did not really appreciate Emily's poetry. His taste in poetry ran to the conventional, and Emily's style was anything but conventional. Her poems did not adhere to rules of rhyme or verse, elements that were used to judge acceptable poems in the mid-1800s.

Emily eventually became infatuated with Sam Bowles, but he was married. Although he corresponded with her, he gave no indication that he was romantically interested in her. She looked to him for help in publishing her poems, but he simply tolerated her poetry for the sake of their friendship. He never really held her works in high regard. One of her earliest letters to him begins with a formal salutation:

> Dear Mr. Bowles.
> I got the little pamphlet. I think you sent it to me, though unfamiliar with your hand—I may mistake.
> Thank you if I am right. Thank you, if not, since here I find bright pretext to ask you how you are tonight, and for the health of four more, Elder and Minor "Mary," Sallie and Sam, tenderly to inquire. I hope your cups are full. . . .
> My friends are my "estate." Forgive me then the avarice to hoard them! They tell me those were poor early, have different views of gold. I dont know how that is. God is not so wary as we, else he would give us no friends, lest we forget him! . . .
> Blessings for Mrs Bowles, and kisses for the bairns' lips. We want to see you, Mr. Bowles, but spare you the rehearsal of "familiar truths."
>> Good Night,
>> Emily.

As the year 1859 approached, Emily devoted more and more time to writing poetry. Sometimes she included one of her poems in a letter to a friend or to her sister-in-law, Sue. In December 1858, Emily wrote her sister-in-law a poem in celebration of her twenty-eighth birthday.

> One Sister have I in our house,
> And one, a hedge away.
> There's only one recorded,
> But both belong to me.

One came the road that I came—
And wore my last year's gown—
The other, as a bird her nest,
Builded our hearts among.

She did not sing as we did—
It was a different tune—
Herself to her a music
As Bumble bee of June.

Today is far from Childhood—
But up and down the hills
I held her hand the tighter—
Which shortened all the miles—

And still her hum
The years among,
Deceives the Butterfly;
Still in her Eye
The Violets lie
Mouldered this many May.

I spilt the dew—
But took the morn—
I chose this single star
From out the wide night's numbers—
Sue—forevermore!

Emilie—

Emily looked to Sue to critique her work, and she usually took Sue's suggestions into consideration. In one letter to Sue, Emily enclosed a poem that she wrote to her father but never gave to him. He had a habit of rapping on her door to wake her up in the morning, when she sometimes preferred to sleep later.

Edward Dickinson,
Emily's strict father

To my Father—

to whose untiring efforts in my behalf, I am in-
debted for my *morning-hours*—viz—3. A.M. to 12. P.M.
these grateful lines are inscribed by his aff

Daughter.

Sleep is supposed to be
By the souls of sanity
The shutting of the eye.

Sleep is the station grand
Down which, on either hand
The hosts of witness stand!

Morn is supposed to be
By people of degree
The breaking of the Day.

Morning has not occurred!

That shall Aurora be—
East of Eternity!
One with the banner gay—
One in the red array—
That is the break of Day!

By the time she was in her thirties, Emily spent much of her time writing in her room in the Homestead.

SIX

The Mind Is So Near Itself

1860–1863

Emily continued to spend much of her time reading. She read some books more than once. She went back to the Bible time and again. Several poets, novelists, and essayists captured Emily's fancy, and she never tired of reading their works. When Elizabeth Barrett Browning died in 1861, Emily felt as though she had lost a dear friend. As with Charlotte Brontë's heroine, Jane Eyre, Emily felt a special kinship with Aurora Leigh, the heroine of Browning's verse novel. Published in 1856, *Aurora Leigh* is the story of a young woman who decides to set her sights on becoming a poet instead of fulfilling the conventional role of marriage. Although her cousin Romney proposes to her, Aurora declines his offer of marriage. She knows that he is insensitive to her desire to become a great poet. He wants only to tie her down to house and family.

Emily certainly related to Aurora's intense desire to gain fame as a poet. Her own career seemed to be rapidly developing in that direction.

It had become Emily's habit to read the *Springfield Daily*

Republican every day. She kept hoping that her friend Sam Bowles would see fit to publish one of her poems in his newspaper. Emily had mailed many of her poems to Mr. Bowles, but never once had she seen even one of them in the newspaper. She had almost given up hope that he could ever help her.

Then, in May 1861, as Emily turned the pages of the *Republican,* she saw one of her poems on the page. She was euphoric. And it was one of her favorites!

> I taste a liquor never brewed—
> From Tankards scooped in Pearl—
> Not all the Vats upon the Rhine
> Yield such an Alcohol!
>
> Inebriate of Air—am I—
> And Debauchee of Dew—
> Reeling—thro endless summer days—
> From inns of Molten Blue—. . .

Emily was working hard at her poetry and under the most difficult of circumstances. The Dickinson home was under a cloud of fear and concern since Mrs. Dickinson had taken ill again. Emily and Vinnie worried about their mother's health, and the chores fell on their shoulders. Vinnie often took over Emily's chores so her sister could have time to create poems and write letters. Emily came to depend on Vinnie more and more. It seemed that Vinnie was becoming more like a parent to Emily than her own mother and father had ever been. Emily looked to Vinnie as her protector, her confidant, and her advisor. Vinnie seemed to revel in the role, and she guarded her sister against the outside world.

In the summer of 1861, Emily sent Sue one of her poems and asked for her opinion.

Safe in their Alabaster Chambers—
Untouched by Morning
And untouched by Noon—
Sleep the meek members of the Resurrection—
Rafter of satin,
And Roof of stone.

Light laughs the breeze
In her Castle above them—
Babbles the Bee in a stolid Ear,
Pipe the Sweet Birds in ignorant cadence—
Ah, what sagacity perished here!

Emily also sent her revision of the poem to Sue.

Safe in their Alabaster Chambers—
Untouched by Morning—
And untouched by Noon—
Lie the meek members of the Resurrection—
Rafter of Satin—and Roof of Stone!

Grand go the Years—in the Crescent—above them—
Worlds scoop their Arcs—
And Firmaments—row—
Diadems—drop—and Doges—surrender—
Soundless as dots—on a Disc of Snow—

Sue responded immediately to the revised second verse:

> I am not suited dear Emily with the second
> verse—It is remarkable as the chain lightening that
> blinds us hot nights in the Southern sky but it does
> not go with the ghostly shimmer of the first verse as
> well as the other one—It just occurs to me that the
> first verse is complete in itself it needs no other, and
> can't be coupled. . . .
>
> Sue—
Pony Express

In September 1861, Emily experienced another panic attack. She wrote: "I had a terror—since September—I could tell to none—and so I sing, as the Boy does by the Burying Ground—because I am afraid—"

Emily was slowly becoming a prisoner in her own home, although she didn't see it as such. She almost never left her house because there she felt safe and loved, and the outside world was too frightening. Emily's panic attacks seemed to be a kind of blessing because her lifestyle became so focused that she had very few outside concerns. Her entire life was centered around her letters and poetry, and she needed a great deal of solitude for both.

It was at this difficult time in her life that Emily began to write poetry about the joy and pain of loving someone and being in love. In the first stanza of a poem written about 1861, Emily expressed her willingness to give up everything and anything for the sight of her beloved's face.

What would I give to see his face?
I'd give—I'd give my life—of course—
But that is not enough!

Stop just a minute—let me think!
I'd give my biggest Bobolink!
That makes two—Him—and Life!
You know who "June" is—
I'd give her—
Roses a day from Zanzibar—
And Lily tubes—like Wells—
Bees—by the furlong—
Straits of Blue
Navies of Butterflies—sailed thro'—
And dappled Cowslip Dells—. . .

In April 1862, thirty-one-year-old Emily was reading the *Atlantic Monthly,* one of the magazines delivered to the Dickinson home. An essay by Thomas Wentworth Higginson entitled "Letter to a Young Contributor" expressed the sadness of a young editor who had to reject so many works submitted by both male and female poets.

"Letter to a Young Contributor" caught Emily's attention. The author knew that women could be fine poets and explained that editors are always hungering for new poems to publish. Emily decided that perhaps her poetry was just what the editor was looking for.

Emily wrote Mr. Higginson a letter of introduction in which she asked him to review her poetry, if he had the time. She enclosed four of her poems with the letter—"Safe in their Alabaster Chambers," "The nearest Dream recedes unrealized," "We play at Paste," and "I'll tell you how the Sun rose." She was so close to her poems that it was difficult for her to know whether they were good or not. She asked Mr. Higginson to let her know what he thought.

15 April 1862

Mr Higginson,

Are you too deeply occupied to say if my Verse is alive?

The Mind is so near itself—it cannot see, distinctly—and I have none to ask—

Should you think it breathed—and had you the leisure to tell me, I should feel quick gratitude—

If I make the mistake—that you dared to tell me—would give me sincerer honor—toward you—

I enclose my name—asking you, if you please—Sir—to tell me what is true?

That you will not betray me—it is needless to ask—since Honor is it's own pawn—

Emily did not sign this letter. Instead she included a card in its own envelope on which she wrote her name.

Mr. Higginson was fascinated by Emily's unusual letter and her poetry. He had to know the person who could write like this. He hurriedly wrote a letter to Emily, asking all sorts of personal questions about her and her family life. He also gave some criticism about the poems she had sent him.

In her second letter to Higginson, on April 25, Emily enclosed a short poem in which she described her poems as flowers that she was presenting to him.

South Winds jostle them—
Bumblebees come—
Hover—hesitate—
Drink, and are gone—

Butterflies pause
On their passage Cashmere—
I—softly plucking,
Present them here!

In the letter, Emily thanked him for "the surgery — it was not so painful as I supposed." She let him know that she would be sending him more poems. Emily avoided telling Higginson her age, although he had asked it. But she did tell him about her family and about the books she enjoyed.

Mr. Higginson,
. . . You inquire my Books—For Poets—I have Keats—and Mr and Mrs Browning. For prose—Mr Ruskin—Sir Thomas Browne—and the Revelations.

. . . I have a Brother and Sister—My Mother does not care for thought—and Father, too busy with his Briefs—to notice what we do—He buys me many Books—but begs me not to read them—because he fears they joggle the Mind. They are religious—except me. . . .

You speak of Mr Whitman—I never read his Book—but was told that he was disgraceful—

I read Miss Prescott's "Circumstance," but it followed me, in the Dark—so I avoided her. . . .

Is this—Sir—what you asked me to tell you?
Your friend,
E—Dickinson.

Emily told Higginson how she had come across his essay in the *Atlantic Monthly.* She asked him to be her teacher, because she wanted to learn to improve her writing. "I would like to learn—Could you tell me how to grow—or is it unconveyed—like Melody—or Witchcraft?"

Higginson, like Emily, delighted in the beauties of nature. Emily had read his four nature essays in the *Atlantic Monthly.* He had spent time with Henry David Thoreau, who had written *Walden,* a book about living a simple life in harmony with nature. Their shared love for nature may have been what bonded Emily and Higginson's friendship.

Thomas Wentworth Higginson rides a bicycle with his daughter.

One of Emily's poems that Higginson enjoyed was dedicated to the months of March and April. Emily had written poems for all the months of the year, but she told Higginson this was her favorite:

Dear March—Come in—
How glad I am—
I hoped for you before—
Put down your Hat—
You must have walked—
How out of Breath you are—
Dear March, how are you, and the Rest—
Did you leave Nature well—
Oh March, Come right up stairs with me—
I have so much to tell—

I got your Letter, and the Birds—
The Maples never knew that you were coming—
    till I called
I declare—how Red their Faces grew—
But March, forgive me—and
All those Hills you left for me to Hue—
There was no Purple suitable—
You took it all with you—

Who knocks? That April.
Lock the Door—
I will not be pursued—
He stayed away a Year to call
When I am occupied—
But trifles look so trivial
As soon as you have come

That Blame is just as dear as Praise
And Praise as mere as Blame—

Emily went back to Boston for help with her eye problems.

SEVEN

I Find Ecstasy in Living

1864–1870

One day when Emily was working on one of her poems, the page she was writing on began to blur beneath her gaze. Emily panicked. Unlike the irrational fear of her panic attacks, the basis for this fear was real. Emily was losing her sight.

There was a history of poor eyesight in the Dickinson family. Both Vinnie and her mother suffered from eye problems. At various times in their lives, their eyes became extremely sensitive to light, and they had periods of blurred vision.

In February 1864, when Emily was thirty-three years old, she went with Vinnie to Boston to consult with an ophthalmologist, or eye specialist. After a lengthy and careful examination, Dr. Williams told Emily that he could probably help her. She would have to return to Boston in April and remain there for seven months for treatments.

Emily returned to Amherst, convinced that she would be totally blind within a matter of months. Although Dr. Williams recommended that she rest her eyes frequently and avoid reading and writing, Emily did none of these things. She began to write feverishly.

She worked late at night and early in the morning, when the rest of the house was asleep and she was free from her chores. Emily had written hundreds of poems, but she wanted to rework many of them. With a feverish energy and the sense that time was running out on her, Emily continued to rewrite old poems and create new ones.

Then, on March 12, Emily was delighted to discover that the *Round Table* had printed one of her poems.

> Some keep the Sabbath going to Church—
> I keep it, staying at Home—
> With a Bobolink for a Chorister—
> And an Orchard, for a Dome—
>
> Some keep the Sabbath in Surplice—
> I just wear my Wings—
> And instead of tolling the Bell, for Church,
> Our little Sexton—sings.
>
> God preaches, a noted Clergyman—
> And the sermon is never long,
> So instead of getting to Heaven, at last—
> I'm going, all along.

On March 30, Emily saw another one of her poems in the *Springfield Daily Republican.*

> Blazing in Gold and quenching in Purple
> Leaping like Leopards to the Sky

Then at the feet of the old Horizon
Laying her spotted Face to die
Stooping as low as the Otter's Window
Touching the Roof and tinting the Barn
Kissing her Bonnet to the Meadow
And the Juggler of Day is gone

The publication of these two poems was the bright spot in the midst of her troubles.

In April, Vinnie accompanied her sister back to Boston and settled her in with their cousins, Loo and Fanny Norcross. Their mother was the aunt whom Emily had stayed with as a toddler. Aunt Lavinia had died the year before, and her daughters lived in a boardinghouse. Emily was close to her cousins. They had visited Emily in Amherst after their mother had died, and Emily had affection for both of them.

Emily wrote to Vinnie about the treatment for her eyes.

> Dear Vinnie,
>
> I miss you most, and I want to go Home and take good care of you and make you happy every day.
>
> The Doctor is not willing yet, and He is not willing I should write. He wrote to Father, himself, because He thought it not best for me.
>
> You wont think it strange any more, will you?
>
> Loo and Fanny take sweet care of me, and let me want for nothing, but I am not at Home, and the calls at the Doctor's are painful, and dear Vinnie, I have not looked at the Spring.
>
> Wont you help me be patient?
>
> I cannot write but this, and send a little flower, and hope you wont forget me, because I want to come so much I cannot make it show.
>
> Emily.

In a letter to Higginson in early June, Emily hinted that she was told not to write for a while, but she had defied the doctor's orders. "Can you render my Pencil? The Physician has taken away my Pen."

Emily did not return home again until just before Thanksgiving. Her eyes were sensitive to light, but she was trying to live her normal life. In a letter to her cousin Loo a few weeks after she returned home, Emily wrote about her activities:

> All that my eyes will let me shall be said for Loo, dear little solid gold girl. . . .
>
> You persuade me to speak of my eyes, which I shunned doing, because I wanted you to rest. I could not bear a single sigh should tarnish your vacation, but, lest through me one bird delay a change of latitude, I will tell you, dear.
>
> The eyes are as with you, sometimes easy, sometimes sad. I think they are not worse, nor do I think them better than when I came home.
>
> The snow-light offends them, and the house is bright; notwithstanding, they hope some. For the first few weeks I did nothing but comfort my plants, till now their small green cheeks are covered with smiles. . . .

Emily returned to Boston in April 1865 for another eye examination. Her eyes were still sensitive to sunlight, but she decided not to consult any more doctors. She hoped that the condition would clear up eventually.

The list of authors whose books Emily considered worthwhile reading grew shorter as the years went by. But one author stood out over all the rest in Emily's opinion—William Shakespeare. After she had returned from Boston, her eyes had improved enough that she could read again. Emily rejoiced. She decided to read a collection of Shakespeare's plays. She was filled with a new appreciation for his writing and felt that a person needn't read anyone else but Shake-speare to fulfill their literary needs.

> How my blood bounded! Shakespeare was the first . . .
> I thought why clasp any hand but this? Give me ever
> to drink of this wine. Going home I flew to the shelves
> and devoured the luscious passages. I thought I
> should tear the leaves out as I turned them, Then I
> settled down to a willingness for all the rest to go but
> William Shakespeare.

Although Emily wrote fewer letters during the next four years, she maintained contact with Thomas Wentworth Higginson, her mentor. She continued to send him two or three of her poems with each letter.

In February 1866, Emily excitedly noticed one of her poems on the front cover of the *Republican*. Free of the intense emotion typical of Emily's poems, it was entitled "The Snake."

> A narrow Fellow in the Grass
> Occasionally rides—
> You may have met Him—did you not
> His notice sudden is—
>
> The Grass divides as with a Comb—
> A spotted shaft is seen—
> And then it closes at your feet
> And opens further on—
>
> He likes a Boggy Acre
> A Floor too cool for Corn—
> But when a Boy, and Barefoot—
> I more than once at Noon

Have passed, I thought, a Whip lash
Unbraiding in the Sun
When stooping to secure it
It wrinkled, and was gone—

Several of Nature's People
I know, and they know me—
I feel for them a transport
Of cordiality

But never met this Fellow
Attended, or alone
Without a tighter breathing
And Zero at the Bone—

Emily was thrilled that Sam Bowles would publish another one of her poems.

In the early part of 1866, Emily received an invitation from Higginson to meet him in Boston. He had probably read more of her poems than any other person in Emily's life. Yet they had never met.

Emily wrote back, declining the invitation. She told him that her father could not do without her presence at home. She added that Mr. Dickinson had also refused to let her return to Boston to see her eye doctor, with whom she had a follow-up appointment. The real reason was that Emily was afraid to travel so far away from home. By 1866, she did not leave her house except to go next door to Sue and Austin's house.

In June, a few months later, Higginson again suggested that Emily meet with him in Boston. For the second time, thirty-five-year-old Emily made an excuse for not visiting Higginson in Boston. She invited him to Amherst, however.

9 June 1866

Dear friend

...I must omit Boston. Father prefers so. He likes me to travel with him but objects that I visit.

Might I entrust you, as my Guest at the Amherst Inn? When I have seen you, to improve [my writing] will be a better pleasure because I shall know which are the mistakes.

Your opinion gives me a serious feeling. I would like to be what you deem me....

Dickinson

For the next three years, Emily seemed to be going through a dry period in her creative life. She wrote few poems or letters between 1866 and 1869.

Then, in June 1869, Higginson again invited Emily to visit him. She turned him down again:

You speak kindly of seeing me. Could it please your convenience to come so far as Amherst I should be very glad, but I do not cross my Father's ground to any House or town.

At last Emily admitted to Higginson that she did not leave her home for any reason, which was not uncommon for well-to-do unmarried women of the time.

Higginson finally took Emily's offer seriously. On August 16, 1870, Emily and Higginson met for the first time. Having read Emily's letters and poetry for eight years, Higginson was eager to meet the remarkable author who wrote with such passion and power. Emily was also curious about what kind of a man her mentor might be.

Higginson expected to find a woman vastly different in appearance and manner from the one he finally met at the Dickinson house. He wrote home to his wife, describing the meeting with Emily—what she looked like and how she acted:

I shan't sit up tonight to write you all about E.D.
dearest but if you had read Mrs. Stoddard's novels
you could understand a house where each member
runs his or her own selves. Yet I only saw her.
A large county lawyer's house, brown brick, with
great trees & a garden—I sent up my card. A parlor
dark & cool & stiffish, a few books & engravings &
an open piano. . . . Papers among other books.
A step like a pattering child's in entry & in glided
a little plain woman with two smooth bands of reddish
hair & a face a little like Belle Dove's; not plainer—
with no good feature—in a very plain & exquisitely
clean white pique [dress] & a blue net worsted shawl.
She came to me with two day lilies which she put in a
sort of childlike way into my hand & said "These are
my introduction" in a soft frightened breathless childlike voice—& added under her breath Forgive me if I
am frightened; I never see strangers & hardly know
what I say.

Emily soon lost her shyness and began a conversation
with Higginson. But since Emily wasn't used to conversing
with anyone other than her family members, she lacked the
social grace that demands that one not monopolize the entire
conversation but also give the other person a chance to speak.
In the same letter to his wife, Higginson described Emily's
chattiness: "She talked soon & thenceforward continuously
—& deferentially—sometimes stopping to ask me to talk instead of her—but readily recommencing."

At the end of the letter, Higginson included part of his
conversation with Emily. He quoted her as saying:

If I read a book [and] it makes my whole body so
cold no fire ever can warm me I know *that* is poetry.
If I feel physically as if the top of my head were taken
off, I know *that* is poetry. These are the only way I
know it. Is there any other way. . . .

> I find ecstasy in living—the mere sense of living
> is joy enough.

In his letter, Higginson told his wife that "she makes all the bread for her father only likes hers & [Emily] says '& people must have puddings' this *very* dreamily, as if they were comets—so she makes them."

The following day, Higginson wrote another letter to his wife. It was evident that Emily was still very much on his mind.

> Her father was not severe I think but remote. He did not wish them to read anything but the Bible. One day her brother brought home Kavanagh hid it under the piano cover & made signs to her & they read it: her father at last found it & was displeased. . . .
>
> After long disuse of her eyes she read Shakespeare & thought why is any other book needed.
>
> I never was with any one who drained my nerve power so much. Without touching her, she drew from me. I am glad not to live near her. She often thought me *tired* & seemed very thoughtful of others.

At one point, Higginson asked Emily if she ever tired of staying home and not having visitors. She responded by saying that she never thought of "such a want in all future time." Emily seemed happy to be safe in her home, surrounded by the people and things that made her feel safe: her books, pens, paper, and family members. "I find ecstasy in living— the mere sense of living is joy enough!"

My lovely Salem smiles
at me I seek his Face
so often – but I am
past disguises have
dropped – have done
with guises –
I confess that I love
him – I rejoice that
I love him – I thank
the maker of Heaven
and Earth that gave
him me to love –
the Excellaure gewords
me – I cannot
find my channel.
the Creek turns too
at thoughts of the –
will sow punish
it – I in
voluntary Bankruptcy
as the debtor say.
could that be a
crime – How could
that be crime –
I n cas escalit me
in yourself – that
will punish, man –
with sow

EIGHT

I Confess that I Love Him

1871–1880

As Emily grew older, her creative energy was directed more to letters than poetry. She wrote to her Norcross cousins in Boston, to Elizabeth Holland in New York, and to her sister-in-law whenever Sue was away from Amherst. Emily also continued to write regularly to Higginson.

In November 1871, Emily sent him the following poem—one of her favorites.

Remembrance has a Rear and Front—
'Tis something like a House—
It has a Garret also
For Refuse and the Mouse.

Besides the deepest Cellar
That ever Mason laid—
Look to it by its Fathoms
Ourselves be not pursued—

In the letter that accompanied the poem, she also praised

the poems of her old friend Helen Fiske Hunt, whose work she had seen in the *Springfield Daily Republican.* Helen was becoming well known as one of the finest female poets in the country. Emily believed that Helen's poems were stronger than any female poet since Elizabeth Barrett Browning.

On July 10, 1872, Mr. Dickinson resigned as treasurer of Amherst College. He had held this position for almost forty years, but lately he had been having spells of ill health and felt that the position was too demanding on him.

Emily wrote to Higginson in late 1872, asking him to visit again when he came to Amherst.

> To live is so startling, it leaves but little room for other occupations though Friends are if possible an event more fair.
>
> I am happy you have the Travel you so long desire and chastened—that my Master met neither accident nor Death.
>
> > Our own Possessions though our own
> > 'Tis well to hoard anew
> > Remembering the dimensions
> > Of Possibility.
>
> I often saw your name in illustrious mention and envied an occasion so abstinent to me. Thank you for having been to Amherst. Could you come again that would be far better—though the finest wish is the futile one.
>
> When I saw you last, it was Mighty Summer— Now the Grass is Glass and the Meadow Stucco, and "Still Waters" in the Pool where the Frog drinks.
>
> These Behaviors of the Year hurt almost like Music—shifting when it ease us most. Thank you for the "Lesson."
>
> > I will study it though hitherto
> > > Menagerie to me
> > > My Neighbor be.
> > > > Your Scholar

Emily sent Higginson three poems with her letter: "To disappear enhances," "He preached upon Breadth," and "The Sea said 'Come' to the Brook."

> *The Sea said "Come" to the Brook—*
> *The Brook said "Let me grow"—*
> *The Sea said "Then you will be a Sea—*
> *I want a Brook—Come now"!*
>
> *The Sea said "Go" to the Sea—*
> *The Sea said "I am he*
> *You cherished"—"Learned Waters—*
> *Wisdom is stale—to Me"*

On the evening of June 15, 1874, Emily and Vinnie were eating dinner when Austin burst into the house with a telegram in his hand. Mr. Dickinson had collapsed on the floor of the Massachusetts General Court in Boston. Vinnie decided that she would accompany Austin to Boston to be with their father. But by the time Austin and Vinnie had arranged for transportation to Boston, they received another telegram saying that Mr. Dickinson had died. Emily received the news of her father's death as an unexpected shock. She took to wearing only white dresses in mourning for her father. Soon after his death, she wrote to her cousins Loo and Fanny Norcross.

> You might not remember me, dears. I cannot recall myself. I thought I was strongly built, but this stronger has undermined me.
> We were eating our supper the fifteenth of June, and Austin came in. He had a despatch in his hand, and I saw by his face we were all lost, though I didn't know how. He said that father was very sick, and he

and Vinnie must go. The train had already gone.
While horses were dressing, news came that he was
dead.

Father does not live with us now—he lives in a
new house. Though it was built in an hour it is better
than this. He hasn't any garden because he moved after gardens were made, so we take him the best flowers, and if we only knew he knew, perhaps we would
stop crying. . . .

Emily.

In July, Emily wrote to Higginson, telling him about her
last day with her father.

The last Afternoon that my Father lived, though
with no premonition—I preferred to be with him, and
invented an absence for Mother, Vinnie being asleep.
He seemed particularly pleased as I oftenest stayed
with myself, and remarked as the Afternoon with-
drew, he "would like it to not end."

His pleasure almost embarrassed me and my
Brother coming—I suggested they walk. Next morning I woke him for the train—and saw him no more.

His Heart was pure and terrible and I think no
other like it exists.

I am glad there is Immortality—but would have
tested it myself—before entrusting him. . . .

After the death of Emily's father, Judge Otis Phillips Lord
visited the Dickinson home several times, and a relationship
slowly developed between forty-three-year-old Emily and the
sixty-one-year-old judge. Emily had known Judge and Mrs.
Lord almost all her life. Mr. Dickinson and Judge Lord had
been about the same age. Lord was a judge in Salem, Massachusetts. He was described by a childhood friend as "manly in
his deportment, yet not . . . without a vein of roguish-
ness. . . . He had a most exuberant love for fun. His sense of the

comic and ludicrous was very keen. . . . He loved literature and intellectual discussion . . . and the more earnest and excited he was, the more pleasurable it was to him." He also had good common sense and was extremely practical.

Emily greatly admired this man and began to fall in love with him. The fact that he was married certainly limited their relationship. They wrote letters, however, and shared funny stories. Emily particularly enjoyed Lord's sense of humor. Emily and Judge Lord wrote jokes on scraps of paper. These scraps flew back and forth from the courthouse in Salem to Emily's writing table in Amherst.

> Solomon Pickles: Notice! My wife Sophia Pickles having left my bed and board without just cause or provocation, I shall not be responsible for bills of her contracting.
> Sophia Pickles: Notice! I take this means of saying that Solomon Pickles has had not bed or board for me to leave for the last two months.

On June 15, 1875, exactly a year after Mr. Dickinson's death, Mrs. Dickinson had a stroke and was paralyzed. Emily wrote to Higginson:

> Mother was very ill, but is now easier, and the Doctor thinks that in more Days she may partly improve. She was ignorant at the time and her Hand and Foot left her, and when she asks me the name of her sickness—I deceive for the first time. She asks for my Father, constantly, and thinks it rude he does not come—begging me not to retire at night, lest no one receive him. I am pleased that what grieves ourself so much—can no more grieve him. To have been immortal transcends to become so. Thank you for being sorry. . . .
>
> Your Scholar.

After Higginson had told Helen Fiske Hunt about Emily's poetry, Emily and Helen began to correspond with each other. In October 1875, Helen married William S. Jackson and Emily wrote to her with congratulations. Helen Hunt Jackson had become famous, not only as a poet but for her prose as well. When she saw Emily's poems, she felt that more of them should be published.

Emily's days were spent caring for her mother, doing household chores, tending her garden, writing letters, and reading. When Higginson suggested, in 1876, that he send her poetry to the editor of a woman's publication, Emily declined. She felt that her poetry had become as private as her life was. She had lost all interest in making her poetry public. But Helen recognized the genius in Emily's poetry and wrote to her:

> I hope some day, somewhere I shall find you in a spot where we can know each other. I wish very much that you would write to me now and then, when it did not bore you. I have a little manuscript volume with a few of your verses in it—and I read them very often—You are a great poet—and it is wrong to the day you live in, that you will not sing aloud. When you are what men call dead, you will be sorry you were so stingy.
> Yours truly
> Helen Jackson

In 1876, Helen wrote to Emily to tell her of a poetry anthology that was to be published. She wanted to see some of Emily's poems in the anthology.

> My dear Miss Dickinson,
>   . . . I enclose to you a circular which may interest you. When the volume of Verse is published in this series, I shall contribute to it: and I want to persuade you

to. Surely, in the shelter of such double anonymous-
ness as that will be, you need not shrink. I want to see
some of your verses in print. Unless you forbid me, I
will send some that I have. May I?

The anthology would contain works by several talented
poets from around the country. Helen especially wanted
Emily to submit a poem that was a personal favorite of hers:

Success is counted sweetest
By those who ne'er succeed.
To comprehend a nectar
Requires sorest need.

Not one of all the purple Host
Who took the Flag today
Can tell the definition
So clear of Victory

As he defeated—dying—
On whose forbidden ear
The distant strains of triumph
Burst agonized and clear!

Emily was unsure about what to do. In a letter to Higginson in October 1876, Emily asked her mentor for advice:

Dear friend—
Are you willing to tell me what is right? Mrs. Jackson—of Colorado—was with me a few moments this
week, and wished me to write for this—I told her I
was unwilling, and she asked me why?—I said I was
incapable and she seemed not to believe me and
asked me not to decide for a few Days—meantime,
she would write me—She was so sweetly noble, I

would regret to estrange her, and if you would be willing to give me a note saying you disapproved it, and
thought me unfit, she would believe you—I am sorry
to flee so often to my safest friend, but hope he per-
mits me—

In 1877, Samuel Bowles died after a short illness. Higginson's wife, Mary, also died quite suddenly. Both of these
deaths affected Emily. But a third death, that of Mrs. Lord,
added a new dimension to Emily's life.

By 1878, about a year after Mrs. Lord died, Judge Lord and
Emily were writing to each other weekly and sometimes daily.
Emily felt safe expressing her most intimate feelings for him.
She saved several rough drafts of her letters, all written in 1878:

> My lovely Salem smiles at me. I seek his Face so
> often—but I have done with guises.
> I confess that I love him—I rejoice that I love him
> —I thank the maker of Heaven and Earth—that gave
> him me to love—the exultation floods me. I cannot
> find my channel—the Creek turns Sea—at thought of
> thee—
>
> ... Don't you know you have taken my will away
> and I "know not where" you "have laid" it? Should I
> have curbed you sooner? ...
> ... to lie so near your longing—to touch it as I
> passed, for I am but a restive sleeper and often should
> journey from your Arms through the happy night, but
> you will lift me back, wont you, for only there I ask to
> be—I say, if I felt the longing nearer—than in our
> dear past, perhaps I could not resist to bless it, but
> must, because it would be right. ...
> I was reading a little Book—because it broke my
> Heart I want it to break your's—Will you think that
> fair? I often have read it, but not before since loving
> you—I find that makes a difference—it makes a dif-
> ference with all.

Emily fell in love with Judge Otis Phillips Lord.

Emily's letters to Judge Lord were intimate and some-times witty, but she did not share her poetry with him. He may not have known to what extent poetry was her life, and he would have been astounded and envious to find that Emily had sent many poems to Higginson and Sam Bowles but none to him.

Emily and Judge Lord did have a strong connection—their love of Shakespeare. They eventually used Shake-speare's plays as a basis for cryptic or secret messages in their letters to each other.

Most of the poetry that Emily wrote during this time of

her life was born out of her relationship with Judge Lord. In the following poem, she referred to the awakening of her love for him. It seemed she had always felt deep emotions for him that in "a second" were stirred into passionate love.

> Long Years apart—can make no
> Breach a second cannot fill—
> The absence of the Witch does not
> Invalidate the spell—
>
> The embers of a Thousand Years
> Uncovered by the Hand
> That fondled them when they were Fire
> Will gleam and understand—

While Emily was opening her heart to Judge Lord, Helen Hunt Jackson was still intent on getting Emily to share her poetry with the world. On October 25, 1878, after a trip to Amherst, Helen wrote to Emily:

> My dear Friend—
> Here comes the line I promised to send—we had a fine noon on Mt. Holyoke yesterday—and took the 5 o clk train to Springfield. . . .
> Now—will you send me the poem? No—will you let me send the "Success"—which I know by heart—to Robert Bros for the Masque of Poets? If you will, it will give me a great pleasure. I ask for this as a personal favor to myself—Can you refuse the only thing I perhaps shall ever ask at your hands?
> Yours ever
Helen Jackson

Emily finally gave her permission. On December 8, 1878, Helen wrote to Emily:

My dear friend,

I suppose by this time you have seen the Masque of Poets. I hope you have not regretted giving me that choice bit of verse for it. I was pleased to see that it had in a manner, a special place, being chosen to end the first part of the volume,—on the whole, the volume is a disappointment to me. Still I think it has much interest for all literary people. I confess myself quite unable to conjecture the authorship of most of the poems. . . .

I am very glad I saw you this autumn: also that you saw my husband and liked him, as I perceived that you did—

Thank you once more for the verses.

Yours always
Helen Jackson

Emily's poem was published anonymously, like the others in the anthology, and most readers thought "Success" was the work of Ralph Waldo Emerson. No one but Helen Hunt Jackson and Thomas Niles, the publisher of the anthology, knew that it was Emily's poem. On January 15, 1879, Emily received a letter from Thomas Niles.

Dear Miss Dickinson

You were entitled to a copy of "A Masque of Poets" without thanks, for your valuable contribution which for want of a known sponsor Mr Emerson has generally had to father.

I wanted to send you a proof of your poem, wh. as you have doubtless perceived was slightly changed in phraseology

Yrs very truly
T. Niles

By the time she was in her fifties, Emily rarely left the Homestead, where she had spent most of her life.

NINE

Blow Has Followed Blow

1880–1886

In 1880, the love affair between Judge Lord and Emily Dickinson was still very strong. Though they were in each other's presence only rarely, their intimacy grew through their letters to one another. Emily again poured out her heart to Judge Lord:

> (I kissed the little blank—you made it on the second page you may have forgotten—) I will not wash my arm—the one you gave the scarf to—it is brown as an Almond—'twill take your touch away....
>
> It is strange that I miss you at night so much when I was never with you—but the punctual love invokes you soon as my eyes are shut—and I wake warm with the want sleep had almost filled—I dreamed last week that you had died—and one had carved a statue of you and I was asked to unvail it— and I said what I had not done in Life I would not in death when your loved eyes could not forgive.

On March 15, Lord became ill but recovered soon after. About a month later, he visited Amherst and stayed next door at the Evergreens, Sue and Austin's home.

Throughout the year, Emily experienced more than the heartache of Judge Lord's absence. Two of her friends died. Then in May 1882, Judge Lord became critically ill. Emily wrote to him, describing how she came to know of his illness.

> To remind you of my own rapture at your return, and of the loved steps, retraced almost from the "Undiscovered Country," I enclose the Note I was fast writing, when the fear that your Life had ceased, came, fresh, yet dim, like the horrid Monsters fled from in a Dream.
>
> Happy with my Letter, without a film of fear, Vinnie came in from a word with Austin, passing to the Train. "Emily, did you see anything in the Paper that concerned us?" "Why no, Vinnie, what?" "Mr Lord is very sick." I grasped at a passing Chair. My sight slipped and I thought I was freezing. While my last smile was ending, I heard the Doorbell ring and a strange voice said "I thought first of you." Meanwhile, Tom had come, and I ran to his Blue Jacket and let my Heart break there—that was the warmest place. "He will be better. Dont cry Miss Emily. I could not see you cry."

Emily received another blow in November 1882. Mrs. Dickinson, who had been bedridden since her stroke two years before, finally died. Emily's role of caretaker was over. Emily described her mother's illness and her last day in a letter to Mrs. Holland:

> The dear Mother that could not walk, has *flown*. It never occurred to us that though she had not Limbs, she had *Wings*—and she soared from us unexpectedly as a summoned Bird—She had a few weeks since a violent cold, though so had we all, but our's recovered apparently, her's seemed more reluctant—but her trusted Physician was with her, who returned her to us so many times when she thought to go, and

he felt no alarm. . . . She seemed entirely better the last Day of her Life and took Lemonade—Beef Tea and Custard with a pretty ravenousness that delighted us. After a restless Night, complaining of great weariness, she was lifted earlier than usual from her Bed to her Chair, when a few quick breaths and a "Dont leave me, Vinnie" and her sweet being closed.

Then, in October 1883, Emily's nephew Gilbert died from typhoid fever. He was only eight years old. Emily and Gilbert had been close, and she knew that she would miss him terribly. In a letter to Gilbert's mother, Emily wrote about what the boy's presence had meant to her life.

Dear Sue—
The Vision of Immortal Life has been fulfilled—
How simply at last the Fathom comes! The Passenger and not the Sea, we find surprises us—
Gilbert rejoiced in Secrets—
His Life was panting with them—With what menace of Light he cried "Dont tell, Aunt Emily"! Now my ascended Playmate must instruct *me*. Show us, prattling Preceptor, but the way to thee!
He knew no niggard moment—His Life was full of Boon—The Playthings of the Dervish were not so wild as his—
No crescent was this Creature—He traveled from the Full—
Such soar, but never set—
I see him in the Star, and meet his sweet velocity in everything that flies—His Life was like the Bugle, which winds itself away, his Elegy an echo—his Requiem ecstasy—
Dawn and Meridian in one.
Wherefore would he wait, wronged only of Night, which he left for us—
Without a speculation, our little Ajax spans the whole. . . .
                                        Emily

In March 1884, Judge Lord died. In sadness and depression over the continual losses in her life, Emily wrote: "Blow has followed blow, till the wondering terror of the Mind clutches what is left."

It wasn't long before the emotional traumas that Emily had experienced began to destroy her body. In June 1884, Emily experienced a nervous breakdown. She collapsed in the kitchen while baking a cake.

> I was making a loaf of cake ... when I saw a great darkness coming and knew no more until late at night. I woke to find Austin and Vinnie and a strange physician bending over me, and supposed I was dying, or had died, all was so kind and hallowed. I had fainted and lain unconscious for the first time in my life. ... The doctor calls it "the revenge of the nerves"; but who but Death had wronged them?

After her collapse, Emily wrote a poem about her fear of the death that she knew was inevitable. She compared death to a child approaching a hill. The child, not knowing what was over the other side, was excited anyway about finding out. And would the knowledge of what was on the other side make up for the loneliness of the journey?

The going from a world we know
To one a wonder still
Is like the child's adversity
Whose vista is a hill,
Behind the hill is sorcery
And everything unknown,
But will the secret compensate
For climbing it alone?

By the time November 1885 arrived, fifty-four-year-old Emily was spending most of her time in bed. She was suffering from Bright's disease, a very serious disease of the liver. On the days when she felt well, she continued to write letters to her cousins, Higginson, and several other friends.

When the spring of 1886 was ushered in, Emily was too ill to read or write. In one of her last letters to Higginson, she wrote: "I have been very ill, Dear friend, since November, bereft of Book and Thought."

On May 13, 1886, Emily went into a coma. She never regained consciousness, and she died on May 15, with Vinnie and Austin by her side.

The funeral was held in the Homestead with her friend and mentor Thomas Higginson and the closest members of the Dickinson family. In a tribute to Emily, Higginson read a poem about immortality by Emily Brontë. It was one of Emily's favorites, the last poem Brontë wrote.

No coward soul is mine,
No trembler in the world's storm-troubled sphere:
I see Heaven's glories shine,
And Faith shines equal, arming me from Fear.

O God within my breast,
Almighty, ever-present Deity!
Life, that in me hast rest
As I, undying Life, have power in Thee!

Vain are the thousand creeds
That move men's hearts: unutterably vain;
Worthless as withered weeds,
Or idlest froth amid the boundless main,

To waken doubt in one
Holding so fast by Thy infinity,

So surely anchored on
The steadfast rock of Immortality.

With wide-embracing love
Thy Spirit animates eternal years,
Pervades and broods above,
Changes, sustains, dissolves, creates, and rears.

Though earth and moon were gone,
And suns and universes ceased to be,
And Thou wert left alone,
Every existence would exist in Thee.

There is not room for Death,
Nor atom that his might could render void:
Since Thou art Being and Breath
And what Thou art may never be destroyed.

After the eulogy, Vinnie placed two heliotropes in Emily's hands "to take to Judge Lord," and the coffin was closed forever.

Emily had left certain letters on her desk with instructions that they were to be burned. These particular letters were marked by Emily before she died, and Vinnie made sure that her sister's wishes were fulfilled.

Vinnie found three letters that had not been marked for burning, however. Emily may have meant for these letters to be found, or she may have forgotten about them when she was marking the others. Those letters, the "Master" letters, were the longest letters that Emily had ever written. Their existence is one of the mysteries of Emily Dickinson's life.

The first part of the mystery is: Who is the man Emily addresses as "Master"? There were several men with whom

Emily corresponded during her lifetime. Among them were Samuel Bowles, Thomas Wentworth Higginson, and Judge Lord. Emily addressed Higginson as Master quite often in her letters to him, but the tone of the "Master" letters is different from anything she ever wrote to her mentor.

The second part of the mystery concerns the dates that the letters were written. These dates may have given some clue as to the identity of the "Master," but Vinnie deleted the dates from the letters. Whose identity was she trying to protect?

The special quality of these letters is found in the intensity of feeling with which they were written. Emily was obviously in love. She either found the love not returned or for some reason was unable to carry on a relationship that would be usual for two people in love. This would be especially true if the man were married. Both Judge Lord and Samuel Bowles had been married men devoted to their families.

Emily wrote with intense emotion:

> I am older—tonight, Master—but the love is the same —so are the moon and the crescent. If it had been God's will that I might breathe where you breathed —and find the place—myself—at night—if I can never forget that I am not with you—and that sorrow and frost are nearer than I. . . .
> I want to see you more—Sir—than all I wish for in this world—and the wish—altered a little—will be my only one—for the skies.
> Could you come to New England—this summer— would you come to Amherst—Would you like to come—Master?
> Sir,—it were comfort forever—just to look in your face, while you looked in mine.

No one knows whether these letters were ever mailed.

They may have been written by Emily for the purpose of writing down her pain and sorrow over a love that she knew would never be returned.

A few weeks after Emily's death, Vinnie found a locked chest in Emily's room. Upon opening it, Vinnie caught her breath. Inside the chest were hundreds of poems that Emily had written. Many of these poems were contained in the little booklets that she had been so fond of making. The rest of the poems were written on an odd assortment of paper scraps, from envelopes to the backs of recipe cards.

Vinnie felt that these poems should be shared with the world. She asked Sue to help her get them published. But Sue had no interest in the project. She didn't think that people would enjoy reading the poems.

Undaunted, Vinnie approached a friend of the family, Mabel Loomis Todd. Mabel was also a writer and was very excited to be part of such a worthy project. But she probably didn't know that it would be such a time-consuming endeavor.

Emily's handwriting was difficult to decipher, and she used an odd style of punctuation, both in her letters and her poetry. Mabel spent many hours and days rewriting hundreds of poems, organizing them according to date, and trying to get them published.

She approached Higginson first, since she knew that Emily and Higginson had had a long relationship. He offered to help her, and he selected 116 poems from the collection that he felt were worthy of publication. He and Mabel approached publisher after publisher in an attempt to get Emily's poems into print. But they all rejected the idea, saying that her poetry was too odd for public taste.

Eventually, one publisher agreed to print some of her poems, but he wouldn't pay for the production costs, so Vinnie

The first edition of Emily's Poems *was published in 1890 and contained 116 poems.*

paid for them. In 1890, the first volume of Emily Dickinson's poems was published. All 408 copies sold within a few months, and the public clamored for more. Several editions were printed over the next few years, and more collections of Emily's poems were published.

It wasn't until 1955 that all 1,775 of her poems were published, and in 1958, the existing letters—more than 1,050 of them—were published. Adding the letters that Vinnie had destroyed, the volume of correspondence that Emily had engaged in during the fifty-five years of her life was staggering. At the end of her life, Emily wrote the following poem:

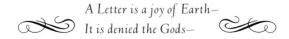

A Letter is a joy of Earth—
It is denied the Gods—

Sources

All letters are quoted from *The Letters of Emily Dickinson* and all poems are quoted from *The Complete Poems of Emily Dickinson,* except for the following, found on:

p. 11   "Emily is perfectly well and. . . ." Richard B. Sewall, *The Life of Emily Dickinson* (Cambridge: Harvard University Press, 1980), 324.

p. 12   "I in the burying place. . . ." Cynthia Griffin Wolff, *Emily Dickinson* (New York: Knopf, 1986), 69.

p. 12   "I must obey my Lord's. . . ." Ibid., 73.

p. 14   "I never had a mother. . . ." Sewall, *The Life of Emily Dickinson,* 324.

pp. 14–15   "January 7, 1838 . . . The children. . . ." Woolf, *Emily Dickinson,* 62.

p. 36   "We may become almost what. . . ." Sewall, *The Life of Emily Dickinson,* 36.

pp. 44–45   "Magnum bonum, 'harum scarum,' zounds. . . ." Ibid., 420.

p. 45   "I wish I knew who. . . ." Ibid., 419.

p. 57   "She makes all the bread. . . ." Ibid., 8.

p. 88   "manly in his deportment. . . ." Ibid., 650.

p. 89   "Solomon Pickles: Notice! My wife. . . ." Ibid.

pp. 101–102   "No coward soul is mine. . . ." *The Complete Poems of Emily J. Brontë* (New York: Columbia University Press, 1941), 243–244.

Bibliography

Works by Emily Dickenson

The Complete Poems of Emily Dickinson. Introduction by her niece Martha Dickinson Bianchi. Boston: Little, Brown, 1924.

The Complete Poems of Emily Dickinson. Thomas H. Johnson, ed. Boston: Little, Brown, 1960.

Emily Dickinson: Selected Letters. Thomas H. Johnson, ed. Cambridge, Mass: Belknap Press, 1971.

The Letters of Emily Dickinson. 2 vols. Mabel Loomis Todd, ed. Boston: Robert Brothers, 1894.

The Letters of Emily Dickinson. 3 vols. Thomas H. Johnson and Theodora Ward, eds. Cambridge: Belknap Press, 1958.

Poems. Mabel Loomis Todd and T. W. Higginson, eds. Boston: Robert Brothers, 1890/1892/1896.

Poems (including variant readings critically compared with all known manuscripts). 3 vols. Thomas H. Johnson, ed. Cambridge: Belknap Press, 1955.

Other Sources

Bennett, Paula. *Emily Dickinson, Woman Poet.* Iowa City: University of Iowa Press, 1990.

Bianchi, Martha Dickinson. *The Life and Letters of Emily Dickinson.* Boston: Houghton Mifflin, 1924.

Chase, Richard. *Emily Dickinson.* Canada: Sloane Associates, 1951.

Garbowsky, Maryanne M. *The House without the Door.* New Jersey: Fairleigh Dickinson University Press, 1989.

Johnson, Thomas H. *Emily Dickinson: An Interpretive Biography.* Cambridge: Belknap Press, 1955.

Linscott, Robert N., ed. *Selected Poems and Letters of Emily Dickinson.* New York: Doubleday, 1959.

Lombardo, Daniel. *Tales of Amherst.* Amherst: University of Massachusetts Press, 1986.

Longsworth, Polly. *The World of Emily Dickinson.* New York: Norton, 1990.

Pollak, Vivian, ed. *A Poet's Parents.* Chapel Hill: University of
North Carolina Press, 1988.
Sewall, Richard B. *The Life of Emily Dickinson.* Cambridge:
Harvard University Press, 1980.
Todd, Mabel Loomis. *Letters of Emily Dickinson.* New York:
Harper Brothers, 1931.
Walsh, John Evangelist. *The Hidden Life of Emily Dickinson.* New
York: Simon and Schuster, 1971.
Whicher, George. *This Was a Poet.* Amherst: Amherst College
Press, 1992.
Wolff, Cynthia Griffin. *Emily Dickinson.* New York: Knopf, 1986.
Wolosky, Shira. *Emily Dickinson: A Voice of War.* New Haven: Yale
University Press, 1984.

with a might I cannot
repress - that mine were the
Queen's place - the Crow of
the Plantagenet is my only
Apology - to come nearer
than Presbyteries - and nearer than
the new Coat - that the tailor
made - the prank of the Heart
at play on the Heart - in holy
Holiday - is forbidden me -
You make me say it over -
I fear you laugh - when I do
not see - "Chillon" is not
funny. Have you the Heart in
your Breast - Sir - is it set
like mine - a little to the left -
has it the misgiving - if it
wake in the night - perchance
itself to it - a timbrel is it -
itself to it a tune?
these things are hallowed, Sir,
I touch them hallowed, but

109

Index

Amherst Academy, 17–20
Amherst College, 6–7, 9–10, 17, 44, 86
Amherst, Massachusetts, 7, 17, 23, 30
Atlantic Monthly, 69, 71
Aurora Leigh, 65

Bowles, Samuel, 59–60, 66, 80, 92, 103
Brontë, Charlotte, 37, 42, 65
Brontë, Emily, 37, 101
Browning, Elizabeth Barrett, 37, 65, 86

Dickens, Charles, 42
Dickinson, Austin (brother), 9, 11, 14, 16, 23–24, 53, 59, 87, 101; letters to, 19, 32–33, 44
Dickinson, Edward (father), 9, 11–14, 17, 23, 38, 41–44, 55–56, 62; death of, 87–88
Dickinson, Elisabeth, 11
Dickinson, Emily Elizabeth: appearance of, 16, 24, 42, 82; birth of, 9; childhood of, 9–27; education of, 12–13, 17–20, 24, 26–27, 31–39; health of, 37, 50–51, 68, 75, 77–78, 80, 100–101; influences on writing by, 27, 37, 42, 65, 78; letters written by, 18–25, 29, 32–35, 37–39, 43–44, 48–52, 55–58, 60, 62, 70–71, 77–79, 81, 86–89, 91–92, 97–99, 103; and love of nature, 15, 26–27, 37–38, 57–58, 71; and love of reading, 23–24, 37–38, 41–42, 65, 78–79; mystery surrounding, 7–8, 102–104; panic attacks of, 50–51, 68; personality of, 8–9, 11, 15, 24, 42, 68, 82–83; poems by, 8, 27, 30–31, 39, 44–47, 52–53, 58–61, 63, 66–70, 73, 76–77, 79–80, 85, 87, 91, 94, 100; published works by, 44–46, 66, 76–77, 79–80, 95, 104–105
Dickinson, Emily Norcross (mother), 9, 11, 13–15, 30, 66, 89; death of, 98
Dickinson, Frederick, 11
Dickinson, Gilbert, 99
Dickinson, Harriet, 17–18
Dickinson, Lavinia "Vinnie" (sister), 11, 14–16, 19, 51, 54–56, 66, 75, 77, 87, 101–105
Dickinson, Lucretia, 9, 11
Dickinson, Samuel Fowler (grandfather), 9–11
Dickinson, Sue. *See* Gilbert, Sue

Emerson, Ralph Waldo, 42, 59, 95
Emmons, Henry Vaughan, 47
Evergreens, 59, 97

Fillmore, Millard, 41
Fiske, Helen, 15
Fowler, Emily, 18, 50

Gilbert, Mattie, 18
Gilbert, Sue, 18, 42, 47–53, 59–62, 67–68, 85, 99, 104
Gould, George, 44
Graves, John, 58
Grout, Jennie, 50

Higginson, Mary, 92
Higginson, Thomas Wentworth, 69–72, 78–83, 85–92, 101, 103–104
Holland, Elizabeth, 55–56, 57, 85, 98–99
Holland, Sophia, 25–26
Homestead, 9–10, 56–57, 64, 96, 101
Humphrey, Jane, 18–20, 50

Hunt, Helen Fiske. *See* Jackson, Helen Hunt

Indicator, The, 44–45

Jackson, Helen Hunt, 86, 90–91, 94–95
Jackson, William S., 90
Jane Eyre, 42

Kavanagh, 37
Kingman, Martha, 50

Longfellow, Henry Wadsworth, 37, 42, 48
Lord, Otis Phillips, 88–89, 92–94, 97–98, 100, 103
Lyman, Joseph, 47
Lyon, Mary, 35–37, 39

Mount Holyoke Female Seminary, 31–39

Newton, Benjamin, 47
Niles, Thomas, 95
Norcross, Fanny, 77, 85, 87, 101
Norcross, Lavinia (aunt), 11, 14, 25, 77
Norcross, Loo, 77–78, 85, 87, 101

Olmstead, Frederick Law, 59

poetry by Emily Dickinson, 8, 39, 47, 52–53, 60–61, 63, 66–67, 70, 73, 76–77, 85, 91, 100; love poems, 68–69, 94; nature poems, 27, 30–31, 79–80, 87; valentine poems, 44–46

religion, 29–31, 35–37, 51–52
revival meetings, 28–31
Root, Abiah, 17, 50; letters to, 20–25, 29, 31, 33–35, 37–39, 43
Round Table, 76

Shakespeare Club, 24
Shakespeare, William, 78–79, 93
Springfield Daily Republican, 45, 59, 65–66, 76, 79, 86
Stowe, Harriet Beecher, 59

Tennyson, Alfred, Lord, 42
Thoreau, Henry David, 71
Todd, Mabel Loomis, 104
Tracy, Sarah, 18

Unseen Trap, 18

Walden, 71
Webster, Noah, 18
Williams, Dr., 75
Wood, Abby, 17, 50

Photo Acknowledgments

The photographs and illustrations are reproduced with the permission of: the publishers of *The Letters of Emily Dickinson*, edited by Thomas H. Johnson, Cambridge, MA: The Belknap Press of Harvard University Press, © 1958, 1986, by the President and Fellows of Harvard College and Amherst College Archives and Special Collections, pp. 1, 109 (E. D. ms. #828a), 84 (E. D. ms. #735); Amherst College Archives and Special Collections, p. 2; Library of Congress pp. 6, 74; The Jones Library, pp. 10, 18, 64, 72; Houghton Library, Harvard University, pp. 13 (left and right), 16, 26, 49, 93, 96, 105; Todd-Bingham Picture Collection, Manuscripts and Archives, Yale University Library, pp. 23, 40, 54, 62; Corbis-Bettman, p. 28; The Mount Holyoke College Archives and Special Collections, p. 32.

Cover photograph reproduced with the permission of Amherst College Archives and Special Collections. Cover manuscript reproduced with the permission of Amherst College Archives and Special Collections, Emily Dickinson manuscript #828a and the publishers of *The Letters of Emily Dickinson*, edited by Thomas H. Johnson, Cambridge, MA: The Belknap Press of Harvard University Press, © 1958, 1986, by the President and Fellows of Harvard College.